A Customized Version of

ENGAGE the College Experience:
How to Excel in the Classroom and Beyond

Designed Specifically for
Lakeland Community College

Claudia Lilie • Christine Vodicka

Kendall Hunt
publishing company

Cover image © Lakeland Community College. Used with permission.

Kendall Hunt
publishing company

www.kendallhunt.com
Send all inquiries to:
4050 Westmark Drive
Dubuque, IA 52004-1840

THIS BOOK BELONGS TO:

_____

TABLE OF CONTENTS

© brushingupl, 2012. Used under license from Shutterstock, Inc.

Where am I?
Where am I going?

You've made it! Now What? Those of you reading this have decided to make college the next step in your life journey. Are you ready to change your life? Well let's get started. College can be one of the best experiences on this journey through life, however, it can also be overwhelming, confusing, and even scary.

This course will guide you through the college process and give you the tools to realize your full potential in college and beyond. Whether you are attending Lakeland to earn a two-year degree then begin a career, prepare to transfer to another college, or gain knowledge for personal enrichment, this course will help you on your road to success. Whatever your reason is for being here, the information in this book will teach you the skills to create a positive and successful college experience as well as in life beyond college.

Going to college can be scary when you think about all that is out in front of you. You are going to meet new people (even some who are different than anyone you have ever met before). These new people may have ideas and opinions that differ from your own. They may look different or act differently than you. That is OK. It is all part of the learning and growing process of college. Learning to interact with and get along with people different than yourself as well as learning to work together is a valuable skill that will serve you throughout your life.

Learning the skills necessary and that work for you can navigate you through this experience and allow you to be successful. There are many things that can impact your success in college including expectations. Students arrive at college with certain expectations including what life will be like in college, family expectations, home life expectations, family life expectations, and personal expectations. Learning to identify the good expectations from the bad and how to adjust your perceptions of each is the first step toward being successful.

Beginning to examine your mind set and your expectations as well as what changes you need to make is not an easy task. Let's start by looking at what expectations can hinder your success in college. Did you arrive in college thinking you could attend school full time, while working full time and keeping your family life together? If so, we need to adjust that expectation right here, right now.

College is hard. There, I said it. Now, let me say it again in case you missed it the first time. College is hard. Your expectation and mind set need to adjust to this fact. The Higher Leaning Commission's recommendation for students in college is that they will spend 2–3 hours, minimally, outside of the classroom/laboratory performing course-related work such as readings, research, homework assignments, practicals, studio work, and other academic work for every hour of credit spent in the classroom/laboratory. Therefore, if you are a full-time student taking 12 credit hours, you will need to plan on spending at least an additional 24 hours outside of the classroom to be successful. So, if you are dedicating 12 hours in class each week for lecture and lab and another 24 hours outside of class each week, you are actually spending 36 hours each week dedicated to school. This is equivalent to working a full-time job. If you plan to work a full-time job of roughly 40 hours per week, when will you have time to study, prepare for class, do your laundry, grocery shop, sleep, relax, or enjoy yourself?

Most students quickly realize that this expectation they have is not going to work out so well or lead to success in college or at work. Adjusting your expectation and mindset that while you are in college, life will be different and adjustments need to be made, you have already made a giant step in the right direction toward success. This phenomenon can be called the clueless effect. All students new to college experience this clueless effect because they do not know what to expect or how to adjust to their new norm and are essentially clueless, until they learn how to be a successful college student.

Fear of this new environment and what will be expected of you as a student is normal. With time and learning the helpful tools found in this class, you can navigate your way through the process while your are balancing school, family, work, home, and personal life all successfully. Now, that sounds like a good plan.

Once you find your balance, there are several other things you can do to ensure your success in college. Learning to communicate and classroom etiquette are additional areas that many college students struggle with. College is different than high school, work, or family life. There are expectations regarding how you communicate and act in college. There are appropriate ways and some not so appropriate ways to communicate and act in college. In college, your instructor will give you a course syllabus. This is your "contract" for each class. The syllabus lists what the instructors expectations of you, the student, are including, how, when, and where to contact your instructor. What your assignments are for that course and when they are due. Read each course syllabus carefully and make sure you know what is expected of you and when. Make sure you know each instructors name and how to contact them, should you need to during the semester. If the instructor has posted office hours, make sure you utilize those hours. If your instructor prefers to be contacted via e-mail, make sure you use e-mail. When communicating with your instructors via e-mail, use your Lakeland e-mail account. Include the name of the course or the course number and the nature of the e-mail in the subject line. In the body of the e-mail, take care to use proper capitalization and spelling as well as a professional and friendly tone. Be sure to capitalize the word "I". **You should consider e-mails to your instructors to be professional communication, and the e-mails should not resemble a text message to a friend.** This is a good habit to get into now and will serve you well throughout your time in college and beyond. In addition, be aware that different instructors have different policies regarding how often they check and respond to e-mails. Ask your instructor if you have questions about this, and do not expect an instant response. Knowing your instructors expectations can go a long way to helping you succeed in each course.

Example:

Subject: COUN 1100 — Week 3 Assignment

Dr. Jones,

I am currently working on the week 3 assignment, and I was wondering . . . .
I look forward to hearing back from you.
—Jane Smith

In addition, pay special attention to your instructors' classroom expectations. Some instructors will provide this information in the syllabus, others will not and it is up to you to watch and learn what appropriate behavior is. Does your instructor mark off points if you talk in class, while someone else is talking? Does your instructor expect and encourage student input? If so, how and when? What does your instructor expect regarding electronic devices? Do they allow cell phone usage? Laptop or tablet usage? Does your instructor allow food and drink during class? College students lead a busy life and sometimes the only time you have to grab a bite to eat is during class but make sure it is OK with your instructor first. What one instructor thinks is OK, another may not. It is always best to err on the side of caution and ask first. What does your instructor expect regarding attendance? In college, some instructors take attendance, while others do not. It is your job as the student to make sure you know what the expectation is for each class so you avoid possible point deductions. Do your instructors mind if you arrive late and leave early? Why, yes, they do! You may think college means more freedom and it does, however, common courtesy, etiquette, and civility are expected.

It is very disruptive to your instructor and your classmates when you arrive once a class has begun. Not only will you cause a scene and everyone will stare at you, (there is absolutely NO way to enter a class without being noticed once it has begun, by the way), and you will have missed important information. The beginning of class is when your instructor lays out the expectations for that day. Your college instructor will not wait for you to get settled into your seat, unpack your materials, and get comfortable before beginning class and then you are left trying to catch up, asking your neighbors what you missed and causing a further disruption! You can avoid this by arriving early and being prepared and ready when class begins. During class, pay special attention to what your instructor writes on the board. This is usually a good indication that the instructor feels this as important information, otherwise they would not waste their time writing it down. Pay attention to information the instructor puts a heavy emphasis on or repeats, again they are not repeating it because they like to talk (well, at least not in most cases).

Ahh, we are only in chapter 1, so much to learn, so little time. Hang in there you are doing great and the rewards will far outweigh all the pain you feel right now.

When we talk about expectations in college we have to include appropriate and inappropriate behavior in the classroom and on campus. Most students come to college to grow academically and socially and it is the goal of the college to provide an environment where these things can happen. Thus, it falls on both the student and the college to ensure this happens. Speaking of behavior in college, did you know that Lakeland has a student conduct code? It is in the student handbook and every student should be familiar with not only what the expectations are inside the classroom, but what is expected of you while on Lakelands campus. Did you know your instructor or any person in authority at Lakeland can file

student conduct charges against you for inappropriate behavior or actions? Learning what you can and cannot do both in and out of the classroom is another great way to help you succeed in college. Make sure you review The Lakeland Student Handbook to familiarize yourself with these policies.

Did you know that Lakeland has a full-fledged police department right here on campus? Yup, you heard me, real police! Lakeland has a real police force with all the power and authority that comes with that title in the state of Ohio. Lakeland's Police Department is here to help you have a safe and enjoyable learning experience in a safe and enjoyable learning environment. They can assist you with everything from locking your keys in your car to advising on how to fill out a restraining order against someone. Our campus is one of the safest in the state and that is due largely to our dedicated police force.

Phew, that is a lot of information to process! By learning all of this information early in your college career, you are well on your way to succeeding with your myCompletion Plan. What is myCompletion Plan you ask? myCompletion Plan is part of your Passport to Completion Binder that will help you be successful during your time here at Lakeland. myCompletion Plan is more than just an academic plan of the courses you will take, it will impact other parts of your life including stress , time management, goal setting, thinking critically, information literacy, note taking, reading, and test taking. We will see how your myPassport to Completion can help in all of these areas as we move through the class together. As we have learned today, there is much more to college and success in college than just the academics and getting good grades. Now let's learn more about Lakeland's resources available to assist you.

Shutterstock/Aniwhite

Your Lakeland is Really myLakeland

2

Welcome to Chapter 2, one down seven to go toward becoming a stronger college student! Can you feel the positive change already?

myLakeland is a tool that will assist you in using available resources here at Lakeland. This chapter covers everything from applying to Lakeland, to tracking your degree to graduation, and everything in between. myLakeland is your student portal to access your information electronically. myLakeland is one of the most valuable tools you will have in determining your status as a student, whether academic, financial, or social. In the following pages, we will explore myLakeland and all it has to offer to students.

Class Schedule

Lakeland's credit class schedule is online only to provide you with the most accurate, up-to-date information. View the class schedule at www.lakelandcc.edu/schedule or go to **myLakeland** and click on "Course Schedule Viewer" on the log in page.

- Get real-time data for class offerings and seat availability.
- Search by session, subject, campus, instructor, schedule type, or keyword.
- View class descriptions and prerequisites.
- See required textbooks and pricing.

Don't have access to a computer?
Computers are available outside Financial Aid, in the Library, and in any of the college's open computer labs.

Associate of Arts Degree

Course Number · Course Title · Click here for expanded course description and prerequisite when applicable. · Click to view full catalog entry

BUSM 1300 - Intro to Business [Description]

This course provides an overview of business throughout the world, focusing on the historical development of American business from the early years to the present. It includes major business functions: management, marketing, manufacturing, distribution, financial operations, and human resource management. It also focuses on business ethics, in theory and practice, in today's highly competitive business environment. (3 contact hours) [Catalog Entry]

CRN	Schedule	Seats	Days	Times	Dates	Room	Camp	Instructor	Cr
10468	LECTURE	7	TR	08:00 AM-09:15 AM	8/28/10-12/17/10 (F)	T 143	MAIN	Golden,C	3
10469	LECTURE	5	M	08:00 AM-10:40 AM	8/28/10-12/17/10 (F)	OM111	EAST	Tamburrino,L	3
10470	LECTURE	10	F	09:00 AM-11:40 AM	8/28/10-12/17/10 (F)	T 143	MAIN	Pedersen,P	3
10472	LECTURE	2	MW	09:30 AM-10:45 AM	8/28/10-12/17/10 (F)	T 143	MAIN	Pedersen,P	3
10473	LECTURE	FULL	TR	09:30 AM-10:45 AM	8/28/10-12/17/10 (F)	T 143	MAIN	Churilla,M	3
10474	LECTURE	2	MW	11:00 AM-12:15 PM	8/28/10-12/17/10 (F)	T 143	MAIN	Gallagher,S	3
10475	LECTURE	1	TR	12:30 PM-01:45 PM	8/28/10-12/17/10 (F)	T 143	MAIN	Lewins,L	3
10477	LECTURE	18	TR	04:15 PM-05:30 PM	8/28/10-12/17/10 (F)	T 143	MAIN	Churilla,M	3
10478	LECTURE	18	MW	05:45 PM-07:00 PM	8/28/10-12/17/10 (F)	T 143	MAIN	Fawcett,J	3
13867	ONLINE	FULL	-	-	10/23/10-12/17/10 (P2)	ONLINE	MAIN	Fox,R	3
13908	ONLINE	FULL	-	-	10/23/10-12/17/10 (P2)	ONLINE	MAIN	Gallagher,S	3

Type of class · Days (T=Tues. R=Thurs.) · Class Time · Dates · Session · Building & Room # · Instructor · Semester Credit Hours

# of Seats Remaining · Click here to see required books, optional books, pricing, and availability · CRN= Course

Session Codes
F — Full Term
P1 — First Half Term
P2 — Second Half Term
P15 — 1st Five Weeks
P25 — 2nd Five Weeks
P35 — 3rd Five Weeks

Main = Main Campus (Kirtland)
East = Lakeland East (Madison)

= Textbooks | [-] = Online/Online Lab | [-] = Hybrid/Hybrid Lab | [-] = Self-Paced
FULL = Section Full | TEXT = Offsite/Satellite | WORD = Keyword Match

myLakeland

myLakeland is your student portal. To log in, you will need:

User Name - Your User Name is the first part of your email address (for example if jsmith12@mail.lakelandcc.edu is your email address, your User Name would be jsmith12).

Password - Your password is your Lakeland ID - also known as your LID. This eight-digit number was presented on your acceptance letter and is included on **all** your official college documents.

Look for these icons throughout this Enrollment Guide.
These icons will help you navigate through **myLakeland**:

mylakeland	Course Schedule	Blackboard	Student Email	Lakeland Library	Degree Tracker	Schedule IT	Bookstore

How to Register for Classes

- Use the online schedule viewer (no log in required) at www.lakelandcc.edu/schedule to identify the classes you want to take. Make note of the CRN number for each class. You will need this CRN number to register.
- You must clear any registration holds (e.g., missing transcripts, missing placement tests, unpaid fees) before you can register for classes.
- Register for classes online in **myLakeland**, in person at the Admissions Office in room A-1002, or by phone at 440.525.7101 or toll free at 1.800.589.8520.

Register for Classes Online Through myLakeland:

Log in to myLakeland

1. Go to my.lakelandcc.edu or go to www.lakelandcc.edu and click on "**myLakeland**."
2. You will be prompted for your User Name and password.*

If you forgot your password, contact the Help Desk to request a reset upon identity verification. See https://lkn.lakelandcc.edu/go/portal/help/.

Register for Classes

1. Log in to **myLakeland.**
2. Click the "Student" tab.
3. In the left-hand column under "myREGISTRATION,"click "Register for Classes."
4. Select a term.
5. Click "Submit."
6. Enter CRN numbers on "Add Classes Worksheet."
7. Click "Submit Changes."

See the **myLakeland** instructions (pages 7–8) to learn how to add/drop classes, print your schedule, view transcripts, and more.

Registration form on inside back cover or download at

www.lakelandcc.edu/register

** See terms in the above **myLakeland** box for descriptions of each.*

myLakeland Guide my

myLakeland Offers You Instant Access!

- Access your student email.
- View/search the class schedule.
- View your student record.
- Register for classes online.
- Add or drop classes online.
- View your financial aid information.
- Make a payment.
- View your grades.
- Track your degree progress.

Log in to your **myLakeland** account frequently for important emails and announcements.

Lakeland Help Desk
440.525.7570
lcchelpdesk@lakelandcc.edu
Monday – Thursday 8 a.m. – 8 p.m.
Friday 8 a.m. – 5 p.m.
Saturday 9 a.m. – 4 p.m.

Log in to myLakeland

1. Go to my.lakelandcc.edu or go to www.lakelandcc.edu and click on "myLakeland."
2. You will be prompted for Username and Password.

   When logging in the first time, you will be asked to set up four security questions that will later allow you to reset your **myLakeland** password should you ever forget it.

   Username: Your username is the first part of your Lakeland student email address before the "@" symbol. Example: jsmith12 of jsmith12@mail.lakelandcc.edu

   Password: Your default password is your eight-digit Lakeland ID (LID). Example: 00999999

   To request your username or reset your password, visit the "Login Assistance" link on the **myLakeland** login screen and follow the instructions under Password Change / Reset App. If you are still having trouble please contact the help desk.

Access My Student Email

1. Log in to **myLakeland**.
2. Click the "Student" tab.
3. In the left-hand column under Quick Tools, click on the student email icon.

my.LAKELANDCC.EDU

Schedule COMPASS Placement Testing

1. Log in to **myLakeland**.
2. Click the "Student" tab.
3. In the left-hand column under Quick Tools, click on the Schedule It icon.
4. Click "Schedule Compass Test."*
5. Select a date (click "Next" to see the next month).
6. Click "Reserve."
   NOTE: Photo ID required at testing session.

Schedule New Student Orientation Session

1. Log in to **myLakeland**.
2. Click the "Student" tab.
3. In the left-hand column under Quick Tools, click on the Schedule It icon.
4. Click "Schedule New Student Orientation Session."*
5. Select a date (click "Next" to see the next month).
6. Click "Reserve."
   NOTE: Photo ID required at New Student Orientation.

View the Catalog

Go to www.lakelandcc.edu/catalog.

View / Search Class Schedule

1. Go to www.lakelandcc.edu/schedule or go to myLakeland and click "Course Schedule Viewer" on the log in page.
2. Select a term.
3. Select additional criteria if desired.
4. Click on "View Results."
5. Note the CRN number(s) of the class(es) you want to take. You will need these for online registration.

Register for Classes

1. Log in to **myLakeland**.
2. Click the "Student" tab.
3. In the left-hand column under "myREGISTRATION," click "Register for Classes."
4. Select a term.
5. Click "Submit."
6. Enter CRN numbers on "Add Classes Worksheet."
7. Click "Submit Changes."

*This link will not appear if:
1) it is not a requirement for you;
2) you have a hold on your account that needs to be cleared; or
3) you have already fulfilled the requirement.

Drop / Withdraw Classes

1. Log in to **myLakeland**.
2. Click the "Student" tab.
3. In the left-hand column under "myREGISTRATION," click "Register for Classes."
4. Select a term (if not previously selected) and then click "Submit."
5. In the "Action" column, select "Online Drop" or "Web Withdraw" next to the course you want to drop / withdraw. If you accidentally remove the wrong class, select "Re-Add."
6. Click "Submit Changes."

View / Print My Class Schedule

1. Log in to **myLakeland**.
2. Click the "Student" tab.
3. In the left column under "myRECORDS," click on "Personal Class Schedule."
4. Select a term (if not previously selected) and then click "Submit."
5. Choose to print the schedule.

View My Financial Aid Information

1. Log in to **myLakeland**.
2. Click the "Student" tab.
3. In the left-hand column under "myRECORDS," click on "Financial Aid."

Apply for Scholarships

1. Log in to **myLakeland**.
2. Click the "Student" tab.
3. In the left-hand column under "myRECORDS," click on "Scholarship Center" and follow prompts.

Enroll in a Payment Plan and Set Up Installments

1. You must first be registered for classes. Then log into **myLakeland**.
2. Click the "Student" tab.
3. In the left-hand column under "myRECORDS," click on "Billing Center."
4. Click on "I Agree" to enter the secure website.
5. Click on "Payment Plans" tab and then click on "Enroll Now."
6. Select the proper semester and click on "Select."
7. Follow the screen instructions and prompts such as the "continue" button to enroll in the payment plan. DO NOT enter an amount for the $25.00 processing fee in the field for down payment, the fee will process AUTOMATICALLY once you have set up a payment method.

NOTE: Choosing "Yes, I want to set up payments" is your AUTHORIZATION to process payments AUTOMATICALLY on the due date using the payment method you set up. You will receive a reminder email.

1. As soon as you read the Tuition Loan Payment Plan Promissory Note and click on "I Agree," the $25.00 processing fee payment WILL AUTOMATICALLY process.
2. Print a copy of your payment plan agreement and payment receipt for your records.

Make a Payment / View My Student Account / Enroll in eRefunds

1. Log in to **myLakeland**.
2. Click the "Student" tab.
3. In the left-hand column under "myRECORDS," click on "Billing Center."
4. Click "I Agree" to enter the secure Billing Center website.
5. On the Billing Center home page:
   - To pay your bill, click "Make a Payment."
   - To set up installments, click "Payment Plans" tab then click "Enroll Now."
   - To view your account, click "View Account Activity."
   - To enroll in eRefunds, click on the "eRefund" tab and follow the instructions provided for entering your bank information and using a bank account for refunds.

   NOTE: In order to set up a direct deposit, you must first have an active bank account.

View My Grades

1. Log in to **myLakeland**.
2. Click the "Student" tab.
3. In the left-hand column under "myRECORDS," click on "Grades."
1. Select a term.
2. Click "Submit."

Degree Tracking Center

1. Log in to **myLakeland**.
2. Click the "Student" tab.
3. In the left-hand column under "Quick Tools," click on the "Degree Tracker" icon.

View My Transcript

1. Log in to **myLakeland**.
2. Click the "Student" tab.
3. In the left-hand column under "myRECORDS," click on "Request Official Transcript."
4. Click on "Academic Transcript."
5. Click "View Web Transcript (Unofficial)."
6. Select "Web Transcript (Credit)" from the Transcript Type drop down menu. (You will also have the option to choose noncredit classes.)

Enrollment Verification

1. Log in to **myLakeland**.
2. Click the "Student" tab.
3. Under "myRECORDS," click on "Enrollment Verification."

NOTE: Current enrollment verification will not be available until three weeks after the start of the semester in which you are enrolled; however, past enrollment will be available at all times.

Welcome to LAKELAND

Paying for College

Tuition and Fees

Lakeland provides quality education at an affordable price. Lakeland's tuition is about one-third the cost of most four-year schools.

Lakeland*
$3,216.00

Ohio Public University Main Campuses**
$9,608.00

* Lakeland's FY 2014 tuition and fees

** Ohio Board of Regents Annualized Full-Time Tuition and Fees Charged to Entering Students January 2012

Associate of Applied Business Degree

GENERAL FEE* PER CREDIT HOUR	TUITION PER CREDIT HOUR		
	LAKE COUNTY RESIDENTS	OTHER OHIO RESIDENTS	OUT-OF-STATE RESIDENTS
$11.80	$97.75	$126.05	$294.05

*General fee is $11.80 per credit hour for a maximum of 15 credit hours per term. The fee is used to cover such direct student services as counseling, career services, admissions, registration, etc. Tuition shown effective Fall 2015. Tuition and fees are subject to change. View lakelandcc.edu/tuition for more information.

- In addition to the general instructional fees and support services fee, students may be charged supplemental course and incidental fees due to the nature of certain courses. Supplemental fees are noted in the course listings available in the online schedule viewer in **myLakeland**.

- The support services fee of $14.25 per term ($4.25 for summer term) is paid by all students enrolled for credit irrespective of the number of credit hours taken. The fee covers parking, shuttle service, safety, exterior lighting, and cultural events; or rental of off-campus facilities.

- Senior citizens 60 years or older are offered a tuition-waiver program allowing them to audit credit courses on a space-available basis. Senior citizens taking advantage of this opportunity are responsible for purchasing course materials and books in addition to the general, lab and service fees. To take advantage of this opportunity, a senior citizen must be certified as eligible. Once certified as eligible, participants may register during the last two days of the enrollment period. Please contact the Admissions Office for an eligibility application and additional information. View the inside front cover for registration dates.

eRefunds

Students are encouraged to register for electronic refunds, the quick, convenient and secure method of having refunds directly deposited into your bank account. Sign up in the "Billing Center" in **myLakeland** (*see page 8 for instructions*).

Residency Requirements

Residency requirements are posted on the college website. A change of address does not automatically change residency status. Proper documentation must be filed, reviewed and approved by the Admissions Office before residency status will be changed.

Even with our low tuition, we realize you may need some help. More than 50 per of Lakeland students receive some form financial assistance. Lakeland offers ma types of financial assistance, including federal and state grants, scholarships, loans, and work-study employment. Visi

lakelandcc.edu/financialaid

for more information.

PAYMENT OPTIONS
(See Refund Policy page 12)

Cash
- In person only at the Cashier's Office in room A-1033

Personal Check / Web Check
- Online in **myLakeland**
- In person or mail to the Cashier's Office in room A-1033

  NOTE: There is a 10 business day waiting period before any financial HOLDS will be released.

Credit Card
- Online in **myLakeland**
- Visa, MasterCard or Discover payment in person at the Cashier's Office in room A-1033

  NOTE: Financial HOLDS will be removed the next business day (when college offices are open).

Scholarships
Students can now easily see if they qualify for any of the many Lakeland Scholarships through the new online Scholarships Center.

- Online in **myLakeland**
- Sign up for an account
- Complete one simple application
- The Financial Aid Office will notify students of any scholarship awards

  NOTE: Financial HOLDS will be removed the next business day (when college offices are open).

Tuition Loan Payment Plan
- Pay tuition bills in installments over the course of the term using a credit card or electronic check.
- Students must accept the online agreement and pay the non-refundable $25 processing fee by the due date. Some restrictions apply.
- See page 8, "Enroll in a Payment Plan and Set Up Installments" or visit the Cashier's Office in room A-1033.
- See page 1 for Payment Plan dates.

Paying with Financial Assistance
- If students have received financial aid award notification via Lakeland student email, and have registered for the minimum number of credit hours required to receive the aid, aid will be applied to tuition charges.
- Class attendance will be reported by faculty.
- Refunds of excess financial aid will be released to students after attendance in their classes has been verified by the Financial Aid Office. This process begins at the end of the second week of the semester. Please sign up for electronic deposit.

  (See page 8 "Make a Payment / View My Student Account / Enroll in eRefunds.")

Students can also quickly and easily apply for scholarships through a new one-step application process in the Scholarship Center. See page 7 for details.

- Indirect educational expenses are the student's responsibility until the credit balance is received.
- Students not receiving the results of their financial aid application at the time of registration should inquire about applying for a Tuition Loan Payment Plan.

PAYMENT DUE DATE

Registration Date	Payment Due Date
Spring / Fall Semester	Tuition is due 1 week before classes begin
Summer Semester	Tuition is due by the first day of class

(See page 1 for specific dates.)

- If you are registering for multiple sessions, the earliest due date applies.
- Students will be deleted and will have to re-register if tuition is not paid by the tuition due date.
- Daily deletes for unpaid schedules will begin after the due date has passed.
- All students must be Paid in Full or enrolled in the Tuition Loan Payment Plan by the due date. A $20 late fee will be applied to each unpaid installment. See plan agreement or inside front cover for due dates.
- After the final due date of the semester, unpaid accounts without a Tuition Loan Payment Plan will also have late fees applied up to a maximum of $60.
- Any check or credit card transaction rendered to Lakeland Community College in payment of amounts due to the college and dishonored for any reason shall be charged a $25 return payment charge.
- The student will not be permitted to register for any subsequent term, obtain grade transcripts, or receive grades for the current term until his or her financial obligation has been met.

Required Acknowledgement of Financial Responsibility

By registering for courses at Lakeland Community College, I accept responsibility for payment by the due date of all college charges assessed to my student account, including tuition and fees, late payment fees and reversals of financial aid. I fully accept this debt as my personal financial responsibility. I acknowledge that non-attendance does not relieve me of financial responsibility for the courses in which I am enrolled and, that I will access my bill online to remain abreast of any outstanding balances or other financial obligations. I both understand and agree that, should I fail to make the required full payment or receive financial aid to meet the balance by the established deadline, I may be charged late payment fees, I will be restricted from registering for additional courses this term or for future terms, my transcripts and diplomas will be placed on hold, and I may be denied other college services. In addition, I understand that accounts more than 45 days past due may be placed with the Ohio Attorney General's Office and I will be responsible for paying any additional fees and costs, including attorney fees and court costs, associated with collection of this debt. I understand that the college sends electronic notifications (email) to my official Lakeland email account to communicate important updates, and that I must adhere to college procedures for dropping or withdrawing from courses.

Financial Aid

Lakeland offers many types of financial assistance including federal and state grants, scholarships, loans, and work-study employment.

To Apply for Financial Aid:

- Complete the Free Application for Federal Student Aid (FAFSA) at www.fafsa.ed.gov and use Lakeland Community College code 006804.
- Students need to apply for financial aid each year.
- Check the progress of your financial aid application in **myLakeland**.

To Keep Financial Aid:

- Attend class.
- Maintain Standards of Academic Progress (SAP).
- Be aware of the freeze dates.
- Understand what happens when you withdraw.

Financial aid eligibility is based on class attendance.
Visit: lakelandcc.edu/keepingaid

WITHDRAWALS / CANCELLATIONS

Administrative Withdrawal Policy

Students will be administratively withdrawn from any class in which they are enrolled and have not attended during the first two weeks of the semester. Students are not permitted to begin attendance in a class after the second week. Administrative withdrawals will occur at the beginning of the third week of classes at 0 percent refund for any student who the instructor marked as an N (not attended).

Withdrawal From Classes

Students are able to withdraw from a class from the beginning of the second week through the end of the twelfth week of the semester. A course withdrawal will be indicated on a student's academic record by a grade of "W." After the twelfth week, no withdrawal is permitted. **Failure to attend class(es) does not constitute withdrawal and may result in a failing grade**. Students registered for courses other than the standard 16-week semester should consult the inside front cover for appropriate deadlines regarding withdrawal.

Cancelled Classes

Occasionally the college must cancel a class because of insufficient enrollment. Students enrolled in the class will be notified of the cancellation as soon as possible and may replace the cancelled class. Students who do not wish to make a substitution will receive a 100 percent refund in the mail. The college reserves the right to cancel any classes due to unforeseen circumstances. Students with financial aid should contact the Financial Aid Office to determine if aid is affected.

Complete the FREE Application for Federal Student Aid (FAFSA) at

www. afsa.ed.gov

and use Lakeland Community College code 006804.

Refund Policy

For payments made by credit card, the refund will go back to the credit card that was used when the payment was made. The refund of payments made by cash or check and refunds of excess financial aid will be refunded by electronic deposit.

Students who officially withdraw from credit classes will receive a refund based on the schedule below.

	FULL REFUND	50% REFUND	NO REFUND
8-WEEK and 16-WEEK CLASSES	During the first week of classes	During the second week of classes	Between the third and sixth week (8-week classes) Between the third and twelfth week (16-week classes)
1- or 2-DAY CLASSES	Prior to the first class	Not applicable	After the first class

NOTE: This refund schedule applies regardless of the date a class starts during the first week of the semester. See the inside front cover for specific dates.

- Refunds will be calculated as of the date of official withdrawal.
- Non-attendance of classes or notification to the instructor or department does not constitute official withdrawal.
- Refunds will not be made for classes in which the student receives a letter grade of FNA (F for no attendance).
- Refunds or reduction of indebtedness for withdrawals after the official dates will not be made in cases of failure or inability to attend classes because of changes in business or personal affairs.
- You are still liable for payment of your Tuition Loan Payment Plan.
- In extraordinary circumstances wherein a student is forced to withdraw from classes after the refund period, a written appeal may be made requesting special consideration. Appropriate documentation is required with such appeal.
- Any outstanding financial obligation to the college will be deducted from any tuition refund.
- If a student is receiving financial aid and is scheduled for a tuition refund, that refund may be returned to the appropriate financial aid account.
- Students withdrawing from the college may be required to repay all or part of the financial aid received.
- You may request a copy of the refund policy for financial aid recipients from the Financial Aid Office.

Associate of Applied Science Degree

Academic Programs

DEGREE & CERTIFICATE PROGRAMS

Lakeland's degree program prepares you for a career in a high demand field or for transfer to a four-year college or university. In addition to the associate degree program, specifically designed sequences leading to the awarding of certificates have been developed in cooperation with industry, commerce, and local government to provide opportunities for people seeking to improve their occupational skills or to retrain for new occupations.

Lakeland Community College is accredited through the Higher Learning Commission (HLC) and participates in the Academic Quality Improvement Program (AQIP). The Higher Learning Commission | 230 South LaSalle Street, Suite 7-500 | Chicago, IL 60604-1413 | 800.621.7440 | www.ncahlc.org

DEGREE PROGRAMS AT A GLANCE

Associate of Arts Degree
Associate of Science Degree
Associate of Applied Business Degree

Applied Studies - Computer, Design and Engineering Technologies
Graphic Design
Information Technology and Computer Science:
- Application Programming and Development Concentration
- Computer Science/Software Engineering Concentration
- Database Administrator Concentration
- Operating Systems/Networking Concentration
- User Support Specialist Major
- Web Content Develop Concentration
Media Technology:
- Audio Recording and Production Technical Major*
- Interactive Media Design and Delivery Technical Major*
- Radio Production and Broadcast Technical Major*
- Video Production and Broadcast Technical Major*

pending approval by the Ohio Board of Regents

Applied Studies - Management
Accounting
Business Management:
- Business Information Management Concentration
- Entrepreneurship Concentration
- General Management Concentration
- Human Resources Management Concentration
- Marketing Concentration
- Parks and Recreation Management
Paralegal Studies

Associate of Applied Science Degree

Applied Studies - Computer, Design and Engineering Technologies
Civil Engineering Technology
Computer Integrated Manufacturing Technology:
- General Manufacturing Major
- Maintenance and Repair Concentration
Construction Management
Electronic Engineering Technology:
- Electronic Engineering Technology
- Industrial Electronics Concentration
Mechanical Engineering Technology:
- Computer Aided Design Concentration
- Mechanical Engineering Technology
Network Infrastructure Engineering Technology:
- Cisco Network Infrastructure Concentration
- Microsoft Network Infrastructure Concentration
- Network Infrastructure Security Concentration
Nuclear Engineering Technology

Applied Studies - Education, Human and Public Services
Criminal Justice – Corrections
Criminal Justice – Law Enforcement
Early Childhood Education
Emergency Management Planning and Administration
Fire Science Technology
Human Services

Applied Studies - Health Technologies
Biotechnology Science
Dental Hygiene
Health Information Management Technology
Histotechnology
Medical Laboratory Technology
Multi-Skilled Health Technology
Nursing (RN)
Radiologic Technology
Respiratory Therapy Technology
Surgical Technology

Arts and Sciences - Language & Communication
Applied American Sign Language Studies

Arts and Sciences - Social Science
Geospatial Technology

Associate of Technical Studies Degree

Applied Studies - Computer, Design and Engineering Technologies
Computer Information Technology
Electrical Construction Technology
Electrical Technology
Industrial Welding
Tool and Die Technology

Applied Studies - Health Technologies
Nuclear Medicine
Radiologic Technology

Applied Studies - Management
Culinary Arts Technology

View certificate programs at www.lakelandcc.edu

TRANSFER PROGRAMS

Transfer Center • 440.525.7338 • Building A-1043

You can complete the first two years of your bachelor's degree and then transfer to most four-year colleges or universities.

Lakeland has general articulation agreements and transfer guides for more than 50 Ohio colleges and universities. Ohio Transfer Module and Transfer Assurance Guide course credits are guaranteed to transfer to any public college or university in Ohio. Check for course equivalency at www.transferology.com or www.transfercredit.ohio.gov.

Students interested in transferring to independent institutions are encouraged to check with the college or university of their choice regarding transfer agreements prior to beginning the transfer program.

Transient Students

Students from other accredited colleges and universities can enroll at Lakeland for one term only with the goal of transferring Lakeland credits back to their former school for continued study. Students are encouraged to submit a transcript or statement of approval from the home institution or they may be required to participate in placement testing at Lakeland. Transient students must complete an Application for Admission, the Transient Student Form, and a Request for Transcript Record. They also must pay the one-time nonrefundable $15 fee. It is recommended that transient students check for course equivalency at www.ransferology.com or www.transfercredit.ohio.gov when registering for classes. Transient students are not eligible for federal or state financial aid. Contact Lakeland's Admissions Office or visit www. lakelandcc.edu/transient for more information.

SEE HOW MUCH... money you can save by starting your bachelor's degree at Lakeland.

www.lakelandcc.edu/2plus2calculator

WEEKEND COLLEGE

Weekend College • 440.525.7510 • Building A-1043

Complete an Associate of Applied Business degree (AAB) with a concentration in general management in one and a half years by taking accelerated classes on Saturdays.

Students must be admitted into the program in order to enroll in any of the Weekend College program courses. Visit www.lakelandcc.edu/accelerate to learn more about the admission and registration process for this degree program.

WHY WAIT? Complete a degree in one and a half years with Lakeland's Weekend College program.

ADULT LEARNERS

Adult Learner Office • 440.525.7824 • Building A-1043

Available to students age 25 and older, the adult learner office will assist with navigating the enrollment process. From applying, enrolling and registering for classes, those wanting to return to college or those getting a later start in college can turn to the adult learner office for assistance.

Additionally, adult students may need additional resources while trying to balance family, job and now classroom responsibilities. The adult learner office can provide guidance to the appropriate resources on campus to help with these challenges.

Lakeland
COMMUNITY COLLEGE
HOLDEN UNIVERSITY CENTER

Established in fall 2011, the Holden University Center of Lakeland Community College offers convenient access to complete bachelor's and graduate degrees from a variety of leading colleges and universities. Built in response to the community's request for accessibility to higher education, the Holden University Center has brought 16 bachelor's degree programs and three graduate degree programs from eight university partners within reach of its Lake County residents.

Lakeland's Holden University Center is a state-of-the-art facility located directly across from Lakeland's main campus entrance. Designed specifically for students enrolled in Holden University Center degree programs, the technological capabilities allow for interactive distance learning, small group collaboration, and independent study.

Classes are taught by Holden University Center partners. Graduates receive their degrees from the institution of their degree program. The degree is the same as having completed a program on the four-year campus. Each university partner determines its own tuition and fees.

Bachelor's degree partners include: Cleveland State University, Franklin University, Hiram College, Kent State University, The University of Akron, Ursuline College, and Youngstown State University. Graduate degree partners include: Lake Erie College, Ursuline College and Youngstown State University. Additional partnerships are under discussion.

Visit **www.lakelandcc.edu/uc** or call **440.525.7535** for more information, including degree programs offered.

KEEPING OUR PROMISE...
to create a center wh
universities offer bac
and graduate degree
close to home.

Stay HERE.
Go far!

Cleveland State University
engaged learning

FRANKLIN UNIVERSITY

HIRAM COLLEGE

KENT STATE UNIVERSITY

LAKE ERIE COLLEGE

The University of Akron

Ursuline
VALUES · VOICE · VISION

Youngstown STATE UNIVERSITY

College Closings

In the event of inclement weather or emergency situations, Lakeland offers an emergency messaging alert system. Emergency alerts are available via voice, email and SMS text message. Visit:

http://lkn.lakelandcc.edu/go/alerts

for more information, including how to manage your account. In addition, campus-wide closings are available on the Lakeland Emergency Closings Hotline **440.525.7242**, online at www.lakelandcc.edu/closings and on authorized television and radio stations.

See www.lakelandcc.edu/closings for more information.

Lakeland
COMMUNITY COLLEGE

DEPARTMENT DIRECTORY

Academic Divisions

Applied Studies Division	**440.525.7085**
• Computer, Design and Engineering Technologies	440.525.7085
• Management	440.525.7085
• Education, Human and Public Services	440.525.7085
• Health Technologies	440.525.7180
Arts and Sciences Division	**440.525.7261**
• Arts and Humanities	440.525.7261
• Language and Communication	440.525.7261
• Science and Math	440.525.7304
• Social Science	440.525.7304
Admissions / Registration Information	440.525.7100
• Phone-in Registration	440.525.7101 or 1.800.589.8520
Athletic & Fitness Center	440.525.7111
Bookstore	440.525.7124
Career Services	440.525.7222
Cashier	440.525.7133 or 440.525.7134
Child Care Center	440.525.7010 or 440.525.7500
Class Cancellations	440.525.7242
Class Cancellations (Lakeland East)	440.525.7411 or 440.428.5500
College Readiness & Student Success	440.525.7492
Counseling / Academic Advising / New Student Appointments	440.525.7200
Distance Learning Information	440.525.7450 or 440.525.7232
Early Childhood Teaching Learning Center	440.525.7196
Financial Aid	440.525.7070
First Aid Station	440.525.7009
Help Desk	440.525.7570
Holden University Center	440.525.7535
Learning Center	
• Tutorial Services	440.525.7019
• Test Center	440.525.7574
Library	440.525.7069
Off-Site Location	
• Lakeland East	440.525.7411 or 440.428.5500
Men's Center	440.525.7452
Police Department	
• Non-Emergency (24 hours)	440.525.7241
• Emergency Number	911
Recruitment Center (Campus Tours)	440.525.7900
Services for Students with Disabilities (Hours by appointment)	voice 440.525.7020 or (TTY 440.525.7006)
Student Engagement and Leadership	440.525.7271
Veterans' Affairs	440.525.7246
Women's Center	440.525.7322

Become a fan of Lakeland on Facebook. Join the conversation with other students, alumni and friends. See what others are saying. Ask questions. Share your thoughts.

facebook.com/lakeland.community.college

Learn even more by viewing Lakeland's YouTube channel, where you will find videos from campus, program overviews and current commercials.

youtube.com/lakelandcommcollege

If you do not have access to a computer at home, Lakeland has several computer labs on campus for your use as well as the computers in the library. Learning to use myLakeland is paramount to becoming a successful student. Every institution of higher education has a version of myLakeland to navigate their educational journey.

Reach High, but How High

3

Motivation and Goal Setting

"If you don't know where you are going, you'll end up someplace else."
—Yogi Berra

College can be overwhelming. There is the newfound freedom, the new friends, the assignments that are all due at the same time, and the list goes on and on. By now you probably are realizing that college is not "High School Part Two." College is an experience all on its own!

There are several reasons for going to college. The majority of students enrolled are preparing themselves for a career. Some are returning to prepare for a career change. Then, there are some that do not really know why they are here. Perhaps they had pressure from family to attend or feel it is their only option. Whatever the reason you are here, *it is imperative to be clear about your goals*.

Goals
S Specific
M Measurable
A Attainable
R Relevant
T Time limited

© Anson0618, 2012. Used under license from Shutterstock, Inc.

Perhaps you have heard of the famous acronym, **SMART**, for goal setting. Goals, whether large or small, should be **SPECIFIC, MEASURABLE, ATTAINABLE, REALISTIC,** and **TIMELY**.

Here are examples of **not** so smart goal setting:

KIMBERLY: *"I want to lose 30 pounds in a month for my sister's wedding."*

NED: *"I have to pass my Math 116 class."*

DAMON: *"Maybe I should start on a portfolio or looking for a job."*

What is wrong with each one of the examples above?

From *Engage the College Experience: How to Excel in the Classroom & Beyond* by Claudia Lilie and Christine Vodicka. Copyright © 2012 by Kendall Hunt Publishing Company. Reprinted by permission.

Goals

Short Term   ## Long Term

- Something that you want to do in the near future

- A stepping stone to your long term goals

- It is close to your grasp and availability

- Necessary to accomplish future goals

- Set up a framework for success
- Help you remember your dreams even when they feel far away
- Give you vision for your future
- Are necessary for a productive and fulfilled life

- Can be broken up in steps

- Is more concrete and planned

- Helps to seek out a purpose

- The culmination of many short term goals

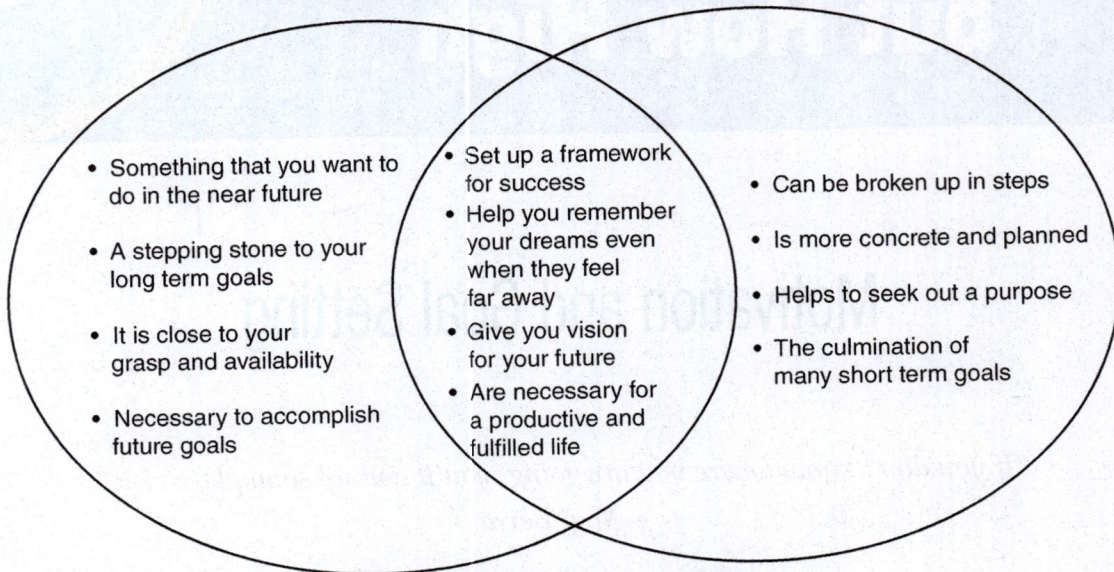

Fill in your own!

Kimberly's goal is not attainable! Who loses thirty pounds in a month? Even if the goal was attainable, she could strengthen her goal by adding a date. Here is her goal revised:

"I will lose two pounds per week by counting calories, keeping a food journal, and walking for thirty minutes five times per week. I will do this by Emily's wedding on June 24, 2013."

Whoa! What a difference! Now onto Ned's goal. Ned wants to pass his MTH 116 class. There is a lot of work to be done for this goal. Ned's goal is not specific, measurable, or timely. How would Ned's goal read if it were written using SMART goals?

Rewrite Ned's goal for a little practice:

Semester Goals

Now it's your turn! Following the example below, write three SMART goals for the semester.

Place a check in the correct category if the goal is:

SPECIFIC, MEASURABLE, ATTAINABLE, REALISTIC, and TIMELY.

Are Your Goals SMART?	S	M	A	R	T
Damon's Example: I will begin my job hunting portfolio by March 2013, and it will include letters of recommendation, transcripts, resume, and samples of my work.	✓	✓	✓	✓	✓
GOAL 1: I will lose twenty pounds by healthy eating and exercising starting August 10 and ending Nov. 6	✓	✓	✓	✓	✓
GOAL 2: I will pass this semesters classes with B's or higher by studying and creating flashcards. or a 3.5 gpa	✓	✓	✓	✓	✓
GOAL 3: Try to get more involved with my religion by reading the bible every night and doing my devotions	✓	✓	✓	✓	✓
GOAL 4:					

NOTE TO SELF: Write your goals on index cards and place them in places where you will see them (bedroom mirror, in your planner, on the refrigerator, etc.). Goals do no good if you write them and then forget about them!

Five Year Plan Treasure Map

Have you ever really thought about where you would like to be five years from now? Do you want to graduate by then? What steps do you need to take towards graduation? When would you like to start your job hunt? Do you want to relocate? What type of career do you desire? The questions are endless, but you can get a grip by completing this *Five Year Plan Treasure Map*! This map contains both short term and long term goals. Follow along the dotted line that you create to see how the ultimate goal is put into action by reaching the smaller ones first.

Directions:

1. Beginning with today's date, start at the X marked "you are here." Write the date and where you are in your plan (for instance, enrolled at CSU for 12 credits towards engineering degree: Spring 2012).

2. Next, visualize where you would like to be five years from now. This is your **long-term goal**. Write in your end goal, including the **specific details**. The more detailed you are the better! For instance, instead of "get a job as an engineer," one would write, "be hired as a civil engineer for the Ohio Environmental Protection Agency by June 2017."

3. Next, draw your path. Some people prefer a direct path from A to Z but others like to draw more of a zigzag line. See the example on the next page.

4. Along your path, add in smaller, **short-term goals**. When do you need to visit your advisor, look into internships, develop a resume, etc.? Be sure to keep with the SMART goals!

5. Sign and date your five year plan to make it official!

6. POST this map where you can see it on a daily basis.

Get Your Priorities Straight!

Don't get yourself flustered! It may seem there are an infinite amount of tasks you need to take care of and not enough time. Make it easy for yourself and break the tasks down. Write down when they are due according to the dates. You can do this on a monthly, weekly, or daily planner, but if that doesn't work for you, try using a priority sheet instead. The priority sheet is a month broken down into four parts: past due, due this week, due next week, and due this month. This is an easy way to organize everything you need to complete by documenting assignments, appointments, exam days, or even outside activities such as going to the gym.

© RetroClipArt, 2012. Used under license from Shutterstock, Inc.

FIVE YEAR PLAN

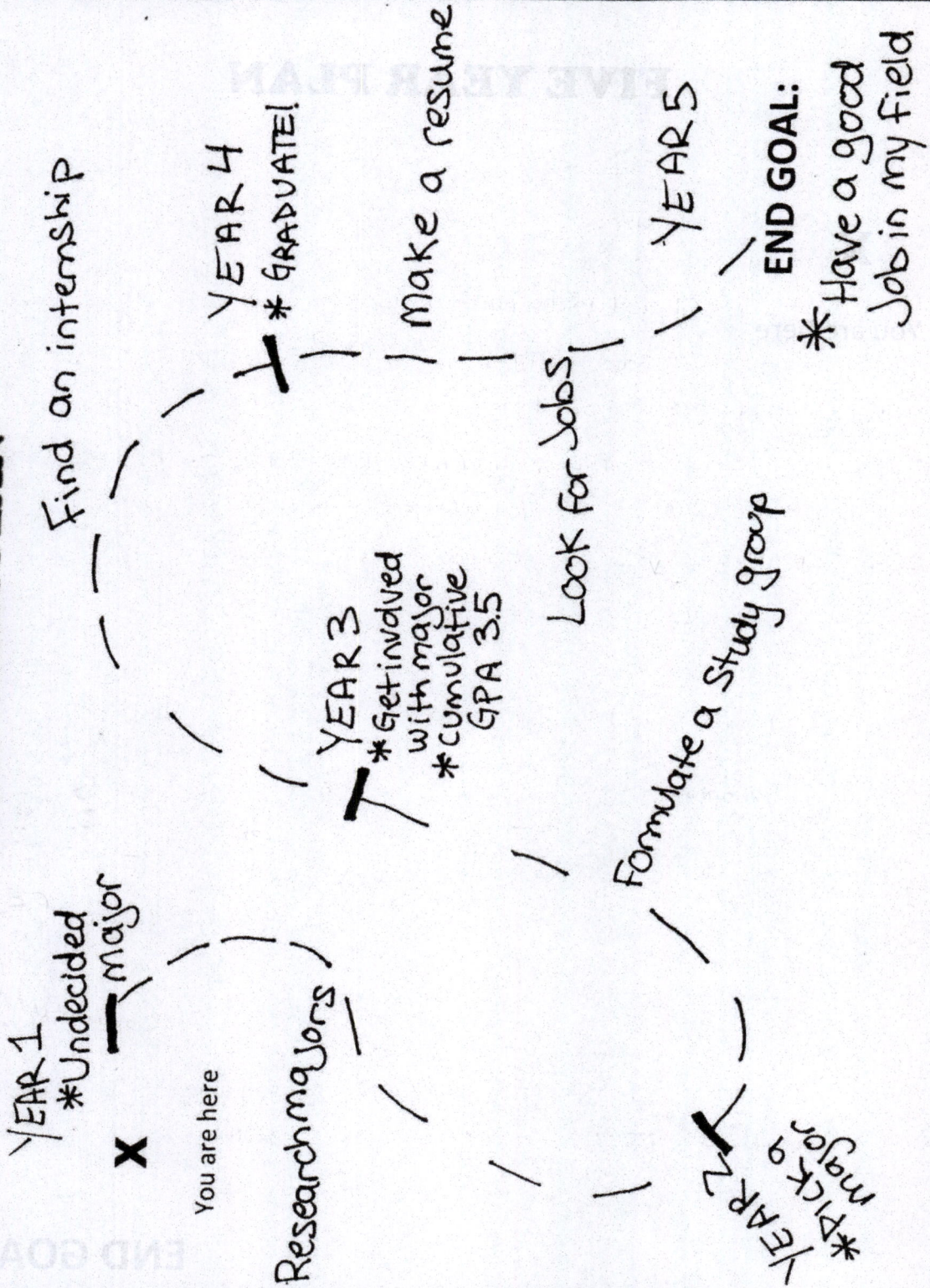

Find an internship

YEAR 4
* GRADUATE!

Make a resume

YEAR 5

END GOAL:
* Have a good job in my field

Look for jobs

YEAR 3
* Get involved with major
* cumulative GPA 3.5

Formulate a study group

YEAR 1
* Undecided major

X

You are here

Research majors

YEAR 2
* Pick a major

FIVE YEAR PLAN

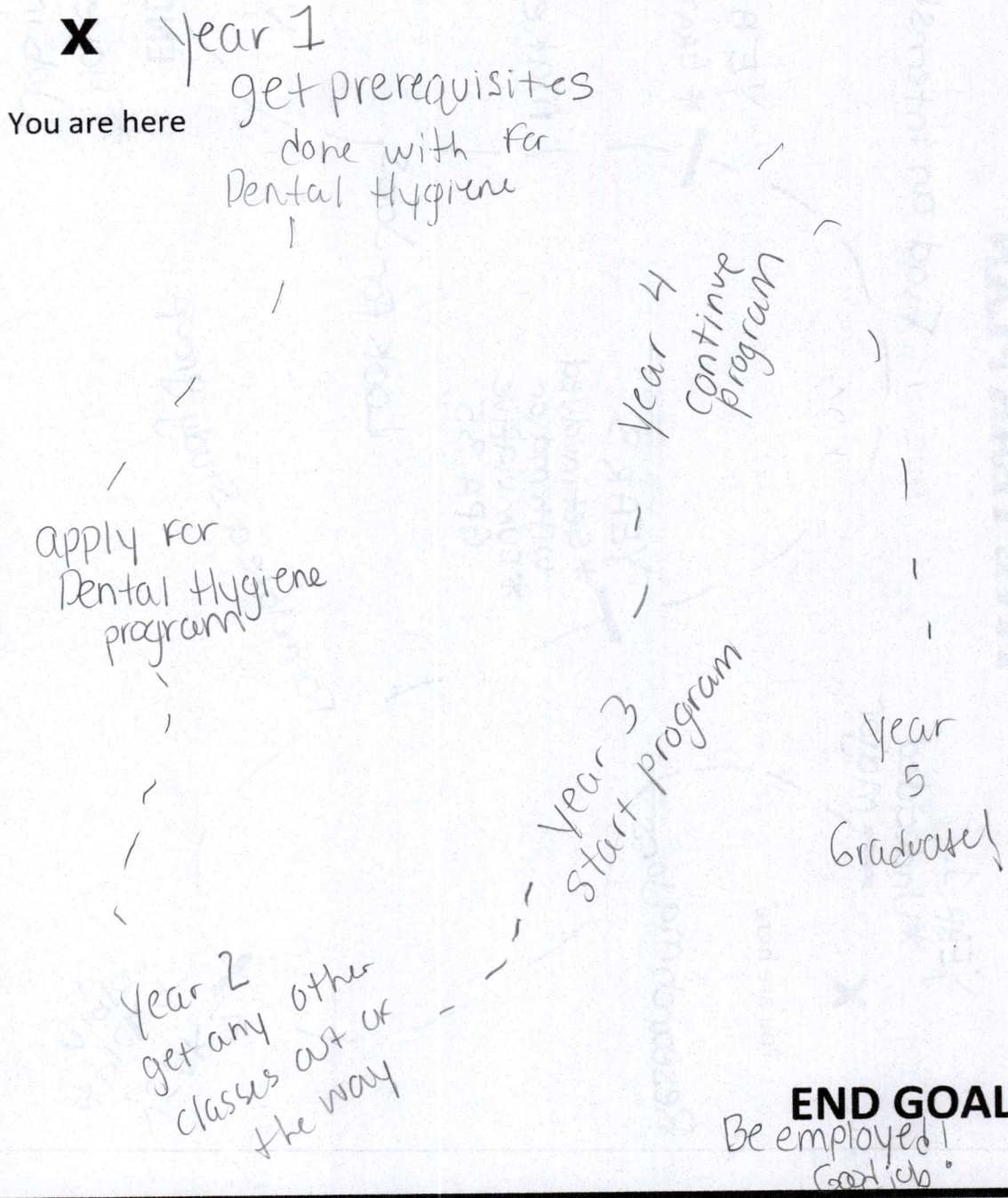

X

You are here

Year 1
get prerequisites
done with for
Dental Hygiene

apply for
Dental Hygiene
program

Year 2
get any other
classes out of
the way

Year 3
start program

Year 4
continue
program

Year
5
Graduate!

END GOAL:
Be employed!
Good job!

PRIORITIES   Week of: SEPTEMBER 11th

DUE TOMORROW or PAST DUE

TO DO

	DUE BY
1. Finish Bio 201 lab	9/11
2.	
3.	
4.	
5.	

DUE THIS WEEK

TO DO

	DUE BY
1. ASC presentation	9/14
2. MTH 116 Chapter 3	9/15
3. Talk to Bio professor	
4.	
5.	

DUE NEXT WEEK

TO DO

	DUE BY
1. Bio 201 Lab	9/18
2. Online Bio 200 Quiz	9/19
3.	
4.	
5.	

DUE THIS MONTH

TO DO

	DUE BY
1. ENG 100 essay	9/28
2. Go to gym 2x a week	
3.	
4.	
5.	

PRIORITIES   Week of: _Monday, September 7th_

DUE TOMORROW or PAST DUE

TO DO   DUE BY

1. Algebra Hw   9/2
2. Chemistry Test   9/7
3.
4. Study for Med. Term   9/11
5. _____

DUE THIS WEEK

TO DO   DUE BY

1. English Essay + Poem   9/11
2. ✳ Medical Terminology Test   9/11
3. First Experience Assign.   9/12
4. _____
5. _____

DUE NEXT WEEK

TO DO   DUE BY

1. Algebra Hw + Pretest   9/14
2. Chemistry lab   9/14
3. Chemistry Online   9/14
4. Algebra Test   9/16
5. First Experience Assign.   9/19

DUE THIS MONTH

TO DO   DUE BY

1. Study!   All the time
2. Next Month: _____
3. _____
4. First Ex. Counselor   10/12 9:00 am.
5. _____

Discussion: Goal Setting and Motivation

When I came to college I thought I wanted to be a teacher. After two years I changed my major to psychology. Then I learned that I needed to attend graduate school in order to get a job in the psychology field. I am having a hard time deciding what to do. Money is an issue and I am almost at my student loan limit.

— Tonya

I feel like I will never graduate. When I started college I had one major goal . . . to graduate. That is it, plain and simple. What am I doing wrong and how do I stay motivated while on the "five-year college plan"?

— Josh

My advisor once told me about S.M.A.R.T. goals and I never really tried setting them. I thought it was just another lame acronym. Now that I am on academic probation with a 1.5 GPA, what are some examples of smart goals I could apply?

— June

Connect Beyond the Book

Lakeland Librarians: Connect for Success

Reference Librarians

You can connect with reference librarians by phone at 440-525-7425, by e-mail at reflibrarian@lakelandcc.edu, or by the Ask a Librarian Live Chat service if you are logged in to myLakeland.

If you are on campus, you can work with us in person too. Just stop by the Reference Desk for help or schedule a One-On-One appointment using the Request Form on the library's site in myLakeland. The Lakeland Community College Library is located in C-3051 on the third of the C Building. Your Lakeland ID is your library card.

Library Resources

Access library resources by logging in to myLakeland.

To access the library's site in myLakeland, go to the Lakeland Community College homepage (http://lakelandcc.edu/).

Find and click the myLakeland icon **my** in the QuickLINKS menu on the left side of the LCC homepage, and login to myLakeland.

Once you have logged in to myLakeland, find and click the library icon under the QuickLaunch/QuickTools menu on the top left side of the screen. Now you can access the full range of the library's resources.

Lakeland's librarians are here to help you learn the skills and connect with the resources you'll need to succeed.

Information Literacy @ Lakeland

The college has included information literacy as a set of skills every student should know upon graduation. These skills will be necessary to complete assignments in many classes you take here. Information literacy is defined at Lakeland in the following way:

Uses Information Effectively

The 21st century learner accesses and manages reliable information effectively and responsibly. The learner:

- develops an effective search strategy
- uses technology to access and manage information
- uses selection criteria to choose appropriate information
- uses information responsibly.

More about Information Literacy

According to the Association of College & Research Libraries, information literacy "is common to all disciplines, to all learning environments, and to all levels of education. It enables learners to master content and extend their investigations, become more self-directed, and assume greater control over their own learning. An information literate individual is able to:

- Determine the extent of information needed
- Access the needed information effectively and efficiently
- Evaluate information and its sources critically
- Incorporate selected information into one's knowledge base
- Use information effectively to accomplish a specific purpose
- Understand the economic, legal, and social issues surrounding the use of information, and access and use information ethically and legally."[1]

Information literacy is a lifelong skill you'll need, no matter what you decide to study or what you choose to do in the future.

What is FiSH (First, Search Here)?

The library has a search tool called "FiSH." It searches Lakeland Library and OhioLINK resources in much the same way that Google searches the web. Using FiSH, with its Google-like single search box, you can search the library's catalogs and databases to find books, academic, magazine, newspaper, or trade articles, and more. Many of these resources will be available in full text to read online, print, save, or e-mail.

[1]American Library Association. "Introduction to Information Literacy." http://www.ala.org/acrl/issues/infolit/intro

What is OhioLINK?[2]

The Ohio Library and Information Network, OhioLINK, is a consortium of 90 Ohio college and university libraries, plus the State Library of Ohio, that work together to provide Ohio students, faculty, and researchers with the information they need for teaching and research. Together, OhioLINK and its member libraries provide access to:

- nearly 50 million books and other library materials
- more than 150 electronic research databases
- millions of electronic journal articles
- over 100,000 e-Books
- nearly 85,000 images, videos, and sounds
- nearly 50,000 theses and dissertations from Ohio students.

Your FYEX Annotated Bibliography

Your annotated bibliography will represent a selection of sources that you have gathered on your topic. You will provide database-generated citations for your articles in MLA or APA style followed by a short analysis (your annotation) of each source's contents. For this class, you will use the following criteria to evaluate the sources you have found: source type, relevance, and currency.

When beginning the research process for your annotated bibliography assignment or any college research project, you should determine the extent of the information needed to successfully complete the assignment.

- Ask your instructor any questions you have about the assignment.
- Identify a topic that interests you. If necessary, discuss your topic with your instructor.
- Write a topic sentence expressing what you'd like to learn about your topic through the research you will complete.
- Set a timeline to accomplish steps in the research process.
- Identify keywords, synonyms, and related concepts.
- Using the keywords you've discovered for your topic, build a search.
- Run the search you've built in Lakeland's FiSH (First, Search Here) search tool.
- Browse your results for relevant sources.
- If you didn't find any results that look relevant, build a new search using a different combination or set of keywords.

[2]https://www.ohiolink.edu/content/what_ohiolink

Need Help?

Lakeland librarians can help you get started with your research and throughout the research process. You should also check out the FYEX 1000 Researcher Starter on the library's site in myLakeland. If you need more in-depth help, schedule a One-On-One: Personal Research Assistance appointment with a librarian.

Know Your Source: Identifying Periodical Types

Periodicals are published weekly, monthly, or quarterly and include magazines, newspapers, and journals. Instructors may require a variety of sources or limit sources to academic journals.

Academic Journals

Academic publications, also referred to as scholarly journals, contain articles written by professionals in the field. The articles may be original research or an extension of previous research. In the sciences and social sciences, they are often illustrated with graphs or tables. They commonly have a list of references at the end. Articles submitted to an academic journal are often peer reviewed or juried, meaning other experts read and suggest revisions to the author before the final version is accepted for publication.

Magazines

Popular magazine articles are not in-depth enough to be scholarly. The magazine may have an area of interest, *Parenting* is devoted to raising children and Time is a news magazine, but the articles are intended as general interest. Authors may or may not be named, there may be illustrations or charts, but there won't be a bibliography at the end.

Newspapers

Newspapers can be published daily, weekly, or monthly. Editorials focus on commentary or opinion, while the news articles are supposed to be factual information. Newspapers may have a viewpoint that echoes their publisher or the audience they serve, which you may discover by "reading between the lines."

Trade Publications

Trade publications contain articles pertaining to specific industries and are of interest to people working in those fields. For instance, *HR Focus* examines issues, practices, and products related to the human resources industry. Trade publication articles tend to be informative and highlight new developments or best practices in an industry.

Periodical Comparison Chart

	Newspapers	Magazines	Types of Journals — Opinion	Types of Journals — Academic	Types of Journals — Trade
Examples	Plain Dealer, Wall Street Journal	Newsweek, Psychology Today, Billboard	The New Republic, The Animals' Agenda	Crystal Engineering, New England Journal of Medicine	Publishers Weekly, HR Focus
Audience	General readership—news, opinions, local interest, ads	General readership—general interest, nontechnical language, ads	Journal has specific agenda written to appeal to like-minded readers	Professional readership—research, analysis, technical vocabulary	Journal of association or trade organization meant for people in that field
Authors	By-line for important staff writers, often no author named, no credentials given	By-line for important staff writers, often no author named, no credentials given	Featured writers have by-line, staff writers often not named, no credentials given	All contributing authors named with their degrees and sponsoring institution	Varies—some name authors and/or their credentials, others not
References	Articles often do not refer to sources	No bibliography, articles may refer to other sources	No bibliography, articles may refer to other sources	Extensive bibliography, footnotes in text, article often begins with literature review	Varies from journal to journal
Editing	Standards set by newspaper editors and/or owners	Staff editors, no peer or expert review	Staff editors, no peer or expert review	Articles "peer reviewed" for accuracy by other experts	Staff editors, no peer or expert review
Features	Photographs, cartoons, charts, maps, ads, and so on	Ads, photographs, illustrations, maps, and so on	Ads, photographs, illustrations, maps, and so on	Tables, graphs, charts, maps, illustrations to support text	Ads, photographs, illustrations

Criteria for Evaluating Sources
Relevance

What type of source did you select, that is, academic article, magazine article, trade article, or newspaper article? Does the source you found give you the "big picture" on your topic or does it deal with a more focused aspect of it? What information does the source add to your understanding of the topic you are researching?

Currency

When was the article published? Would that date of publication be current enough to provide up-to-date information? How might the date of publication impact the value of the information in the source?

Authority

Is the individual or group responsible for the information qualified to provide that information? What are their qualifications? Do they have credentials, such as advanced degrees? Are they affiliated with any reputable organizations?

Intended Audience

For whom did the author or organization produce the source (students, general public, scholars, specialized professionals, etc.)? Are the level, tone, and presentation of the material/information appropriate for your needs?

Purpose

Information can be produced to sell something, entertain, inform, advocate, argue, and so on. In some cases it may even be created for malicious purposes. Being aware of the purpose of the information you're reviewing is a good way to begin to determine its bias and its reliability.

Accuracy

Does the source contain references to support statements and/or statistical information? Are the references relevant to the topic? If the source is a webpage or web document, do the links appear to be related to the topic? What is the source's bias or does it appear to be neutral? If it is biased, does it exhibit an extreme level of bias?

Accessibility

The availability of information impacts its potential usefulness. Is the information available for free or is there a fee? Is it available to the general public or must you have a login to use it, such as for myLakeland? If the source is a website, is it difficult to use for some reason (i.e., congested with text and graphics, no clear navigation, requires special software downloads)?

Academic Integrity

Citing your sources helps you avoid plagiarizing. In the Student Conduct Code (Section D Academic Misconduct 2b), Lakeland defines plagiarism as:

the act of submitting the words, ideas, or work of another as one's own for any academic exercise. Examples of plagiarism include, but are not limited to:

i.   Failing to provide adequate citations to the sources for ideas, words, images, sounds, and any other supporting material for any academic exercise. A citation tells the reader where the information came from;

ii. Copying and pasting, downloading, or importing any electronic material into work submitted for academic assessment without citing its source;

iii. Using copyrighted material in violation of U.S. Copyright law.

When you find a useful article on your topic for the FYEX annotated bibliography, you will retrieve the database-generated citation in either the MLA or APA style. Generally, when working on a research project, you should get in the habit of saving the citation information (author, title, publisher, etc.) for any source you might use to ensure you have the proper documentation. A good citation also helps your readers or other scholars easily find the information source you've referred to in your text.

Connect @ your LIBRARY

Library Services

- Access your "myLibrary Account" through myLakeland
- One-On-One: Personal Research Assistance
- Help from a librarian via chat, as available
- Walk-in reference assistance
- Microsoft Office Suite on all computers
- Laptops and iPads
- Course reserves (many textbooks for in-library use)
- Photocopiers
- Scan to e-mail as .pdf on photocopier
- Fax machine

- DVD viewing stations
- Book discussion group
- Educational and informational displays
- Quiet study room
- Group study rooms
- Collaboration Stations with monitors and laptop/iPad connections
- Wireless Internet access
- Lakeland ID cards made
- Films On Demand streaming videos
- Kirtland Public Library Leisure Reading Collection

Reference and Instruction Services

- Walk-Up Reference

  Librarians are available on a walk-up basis to provide assistance with information searches.

- One-On-One: Personal Research Assistance

  Individual appointments can be made in advance for more thorough One-On-One help. Call 440-525-7425 to schedule or for more information.

- Research Databases

  There are over a 150 research databases available from the library. These databases contain many diverse items, including but not limited to e-books, articles, audio recordings, and streaming videos.

- Course/Textbook Reserves

  Supplemental course materials and select textbooks are available to students at the Circulation Desk for use in the library.

- Periodicals

  Periodical titles are available in print and electronically. The current print issue does not circulate. Past issues can be checked out for one week.

- Newspapers

  Local and national newspapers are available in the library.

Test This!

"What do I want to be when I . . .?"
—Unknown

You tell everyone you have decided to attend Lakekand Community College and the first response and question you probably hear is, "Awesome! What is your major?" For some students, this is an easy question to answer. For others, the thought of choosing a major is overwhelming.

Perhaps you fit into one of the following categories:

✔ **Undecided**—*I marked undecided on my admission application for major.*

(Note: 30% of incoming freshman students who are admitted to Cleveland State University mark this on their application.)

© PHOTOBUAY, 2012. Used under license from Shutterstock, Inc.

✔ **Obligated to make a decision**—*I felt obligated to choose a major so I marked _____. Now I have no interest in that major.*

✔ **Mid semester change**—*I thought I would like _____ as a major. I went to see my advisor and have changed majors.*

✔ **I knew it all along**—*I knew my major in high school and am very happy with my choice.*

Am I on the Right Track?

Yes, all the students above are on the right track. During your freshman year and even up to 60 credit hours, it is OK to change your major. The sooner you find the one that fits you, the easier it will be to complete your degree in four years. As long as you keep your advisor informed and let them assist you in making the correct choice for you, they will guide you down the path to earning your degree.

What is a Major?

Your major should be something you are passionate about. It is also the area of study that you are most focused on in college. Some examples of majors are Electrical Engineering, Nursing, Marketing, Economics, and Middle Childhood Education.

How do I Start?

Look at your personal values by considering these questions.

Where do you want to work? What hours do you want to work? Do you have a desire to travel in your job? Do you like to work with people or do you prefer to work in a lab with data? Just because a friend or family member says this is a great career does not mean it is the one for you.

Reflect on the following statements:

My strengths are . . .

My weaknesses are . . .

I have an interest in . . .

I am skilled at . . .

I have trouble completing . . .

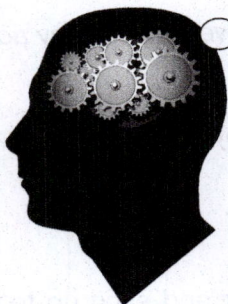

Which statements indicate you should *not* pursue a particular major in this area? Remember, you should enjoy doing this every day. A major or minor that causes you to procrastinate or distress is not for you.

Start exploring the areas you are excited about. Talk to someone in the profession; research the careers in this area, shadow a person, talk to a student in the major, or talk to your advisor.

Work Value Inventory

When considering a major, think about the values you want in your career after you graduate. Is family time important? Do you want a job where you travel? What is important to you?

List 8 values that are important to you when choosing a major and later in a career.

1.

2.

3.

4.

5.

6.

7.

8.

Topics to Brainstorm Ideas

Culture
Challenging
Freedom
Family
Independence
Income

Helping Others
Leisure
Love
Security
Success
Variety

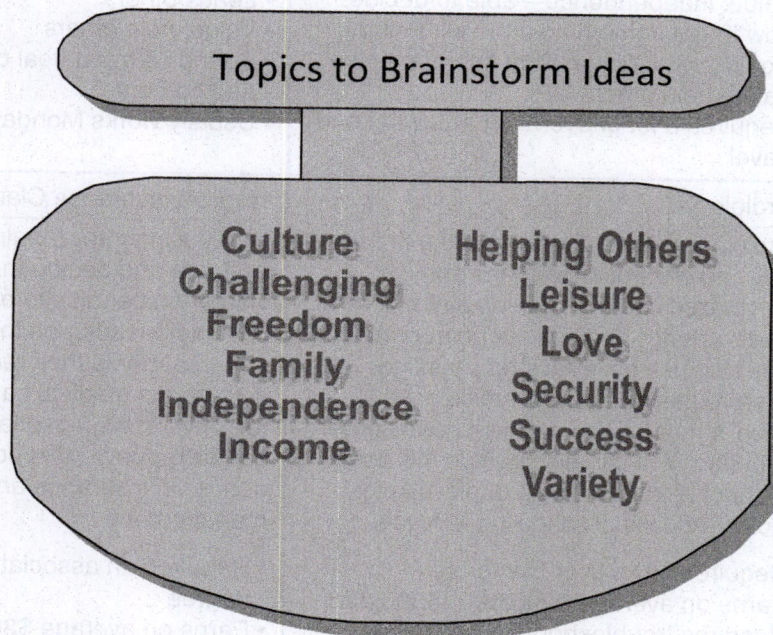

Based on the Daniel E. Super's Work Value Inventory (1970) and the Maryland Work Value Inventory

Questions to Consider

How well do your values correspond to a major in Psychology or Allied Health?

What values from these job descriptions match your values?

Psychology Major	**Admissions Counselor** Responsible for the recruitment and enrollment of students to a college or university. Admission Counselors are typically assigned to a particular geographic territory. The Counselor will balance his/her efforts between individual entrepreneurship and support of the admissions team. You can also pursue this position with a degree in education, higher education administration, or counseling. • Requires a bachelor's degree • Earns on average $45,000 • Requires good listening skills and the ability to be aware of the reactions of others • Requires good negotiating skills • Value: independence—able to decide how to get something done without the significant direction from someone else • Value: help others • Requires a lot of overnight and weekend travel	**Employee Training Instructor** They develop course materials and train employees in job skills and decision making skills needed to enhance their job performance and career development within an organization. They select and develop teaching aids. Assess trainees to determine their skill level and their training needs. You can also pursue this position with a degree in education, human resources, business, or organizational administration and leadership. • Requires a bachelor's or master's degree • Earns on average $39,000–$68,000 • Requires you to give speeches and talk to groups of people, to teach others, and use logic to identify strengths and weaknesses of solutions • Leads others • Value: help others • Spends a great deal of time on phone and computer • Usually works Monday–Friday, 8–5
Allied Health Major	**Cardiologist** Cardiologists treat diseases of the heart. They use electrocardiograms and miniaturized cameras inserted into the heart's arteries to diagnose heart problems. They also use physical stress tests to measure the impact of exercise on the patient's heart. They decide if heart surgery is needed. You can also pursue this position with bachelors in biology, or pre-medical studies. Additional schooling is required. • Requires a Ph. D or Doctorate • Earns on average $200,000–$300,000 • Requires troubleshooting, problem solving, and science skills • Accuracy is a must in this profession. There are serious consequences for errors made. • Values: help others, high income, independence, prestige • Will be exposed to diseases and infections • Hours vary. Works nights and weekends.	**Medical Insurance Claims Analyst** Medical insurance claims analysts evaluate and decide the amount of insurance benefits to be paid to medical patients based upon the medical diagnosis and treatments they received. For ambiguous medical cases, they contact the physicians, hospitals, or patients. You can also pursue this position with a degree in insurance and risk management. • Requires an associate or bachelor's degree • Earns on average $30,000–$45,000 • Requires negotiating and persuasion skills • Value: stability—duties of job are stable and predictable • On the phone and computer most of the day • Will be put in situations with potential conflict • Typically works Monday–Friday, 8–5

Scenario 1: Lorna's Dilemma

Lorna is a full time student living in the residence halls. After two years of college, she has narrowed down her major to music and engineering. All her general education requirements have been completed and it is time to make the choice. When choosing general education courses she completed several of the courses in music, math and physics. Growing up, Lorna enjoyed taking courses in math and science. She enjoyed the discovery of new ideas. To her, math and science were easy to understand and apply to new concepts. She spent her summers playing in a jazz band for local summer festivals. In school she was involved in band and jazz band. She practiced hours on several instruments and always brought home top honors when entered into a school instrumental contest. Lorna enjoys taking her family's old equipment apart to see how it works.

© nuttakit, 2012. Used under license from Shutterstock, Inc.

Lorna cannot decide which major to choose. She enjoys both music and engineering. Lorna is living in the residence halls to become independent, even though her family is 30 minutes away. She wants to have a secure future that involves doing interesting work. Lorna does not want a job that does the same thing day after day. She wants to do something that makes a difference but also allows her to relax and do things she enjoys outside of work.

Questions to Consider

For each of the scenarios below:

What are the student's strengths and weaknesses?

What skills does the student possess?

What ideals are important to the student?

What major should the student consider?

Scenario 2: Enrique's Dilemma

Enrique and Rita married young and have two children ages six and eight. Spending time with their children and family are important to both of them. For the last several years, Enrique has been working full time to support his family and to provide an income while Rita attended college to complete her degree. It is now Enrique's time to finish his education. He plans on working full time and going to school part time. Rita's new job requires her to travel several weeks out of the year. During these times, Enrique is both father and mother to the children, on top of work and school. Enrique was able to complete the courses and practicum experience to work as a lab assistant at a local hospital. The hours worked well with the family when Rita was in school. Enrique's salary paid the bills, but not anymore.

The natural fit would be for Enrique to pursue a degree in the medical field. He wishes he could find something that fit his interests of owning his own restaurant. Food has always been the main focus at all family events. He enjoys making meals for his children from his childhood. Carrying on the ethnic traditions of his family is important to him. It is risky to start your own restaurant. Many fail in the first year. He ponders whether he should look into business or a culinary degree. Which would be more helpful? Then again, he already has a job in the health field and could advance quickly with a four year degree. . . .

Additional Resources to Further Explore Your Major and Career Options

Career Services Center—A place to further explore career options related to majors offered at Lakeland Community College . Visit here to look into internships, co-op opportunities, campus employment, and to discuss career opportunities after graduation.

visit the LCC Career Services Center on the Lakeland website.

O*NET Online—Database and interactive application to explore different occupations. It is sponsored by the US Department of Labor and a great source for career exploration. O*NET will assist students in self-assessment and exploration of careers through online assessments.

Access O*NET at *http://www.onetcenter.org*

ADVISOR VISIT

Use this handy worksheet to help you plan your next trip to your advisor. Don't forget to take notes while you are there!

BEFORE THE VISIT

Advisor Name: _____

Advisor Email: _____ Phone:_____

Date of visit: _____ Time of visit: _____

Location: _____

Reason for visit: (check all that apply)

☐ Discuss my major/change of major

☐ Plan courses for next semester

☐ To discuss a problem or concern

☐ To plan for graduation

☐ To discuss course requirements/goals/grades

☐ Other:_____

What questions will you ask during the visit?

1. _____

2. _____

3. _____

4. _____

DURING THE VISIT

While meeting with your advisor, take notes on the **back** of this worksheet. Be sure to write the answers to your questions.

Answers to my questions:

_____

Advisor advice:

_____

Things to do:

1. _____
2. _____
3. _____

_____

Schedule your next visit...

Date of next visit:_____

Time of next visit:_____

ADVISING VERIFICATION

Advisor Name: _____ College: _____

Advisor Signature: _____ Date: _____

Discussion

I am taking a lot of general education requirements. How do I know if they apply to my major?

– Matt

My Mom really wants me to be a nurse, but I hate biology. What should I do?

– Shaunte

It is my senior year and I am seriously considering changing my major. Am I crazy?

– Sean

This is Only a Test

Exam Preparation and Anxiety Management

"Education is not the learning of facts, but the training of the mind to think."
–Albert Einstein

Sure, you would rather do anything than take an exam. You may doubt your knowledge or study skills. Perhaps you have struggled with test taking in the past. With the following tips for **before, during, and after the exam**, you can develop a plan for success! Which tips have you tried? *Which new tips will you try?*

Before the Test

- Schedule your study sessions well in advance. Begin to study *at least* two weeks prior to each exam. It is important to avoid cramming. Cramming leads to anxiety which may hinder your test performance.
- Be sure you know exactly *when* the test will be, what *format* it will be (multiple choice, essay, fill in), what *chapters* the test will cover, as well as how long you have to take it.
- Come prepared. Do you have the materials you need?
- Eat a nutritious breakfast and arrive early to the exam.
- Wear a watch to monitor your progress.
- Have a POSITIVE ATTITUDE! If you go in telling yourself, *"I am going to fail this"* you will not do so hot. Repeat to yourself an affirmation such as *"I am prepared and ready to do my best!"*

During the Test

- Read the directions very carefully!
- Make the test your own! Skim the entire test and start with a question you are comfortable with.
- Use the process of elimination. Ask if you are allowed to write on the test. Look for the wrong answers first and cross them out. Narrow down your choices.
- Do a "brain dump"; once you get your exam, jot down any formulas or terms you are trying to remember.

- Try covering up the answers. Read the question, determine the answer, and then select the answer that best fits your understanding.
- If you are unsure about a question, be sure to ask the professor.
- Take your time. Remember that test taking is NOT a race!

After the Test

- Check your work prior to turning in the test.
- Once returned, file it away with the notes from that test. You may need to refer to these items in the future, especially if the exam is cumulative.
- Talk with your professor about any questions or concerns you may have.
- Learn from your mistakes and missed questions. Try to avoid making similar mistakes on the next exam.
- Begin to study and create study guides for the next exam.
- Reward yourself for a job well done (if it *was* a job well done, that is). Cupcakes usually do the trick.

Test Anxiety

A certain amount of anxiety before a test is OK—in fact, it can be beneficial and give you that jolt of adrenaline to help you perform better on the exam. But like anything else, too much of a good thing is too much! Too much anxiety can create physical and mental problems, which will hurt your chances of doing well on the exam. In addition, eating right, sleeping right, getting some exercise, scheduling study time and taking breaks after 20–30 minutes of study will go a long way to reduce stress and increase your performance on exams. If you find your anxiety increasing, talk with someone. Sometimes the right person can help us clarify our thoughts and clear up some misconceptions about exams!

Here are some quick suggestions to help battle test anxiety:

- Breathe deeply. Take three long, calming breaths in through your nose and out through your mouth.
- Develop and recite a positive affirmation for test taking. This will help you keep the test in perspective.

- ○ In the restroom or some other private space, shake out your arms and legs. This looks a little funny but it works!
- ○ Listen to relaxing music or a song that makes you feel confident and ready to take control, such as "Eye of the Tiger" by Survivor.

Stress Management

Ahhhhhh!!!!! My life is falling apart! My life is falling apart!
By: Erin Hanrahan, English 101 SLA Leader and CSU student

Stop! Right there. Stop. Inhale deeply. Hold it for a minute. Release it. No, I don't hold a Bachelor of Arts in Yoga or Relaxation Techniques. It's an old trick and people have been giving each other that little tidbit of advice for years for a reason.

Also, stop and think. Make a plan for managing your life and follow it through as much as you can. Academia, regardless of where you intend to go with it—be it a Bachelors degree, then a career, or a Masters degree, then a career—can be all consuming. Manage your academic life appropriately to maximize your chances of success, but also make a healthy amount of time for those aspects outside of your academic life.

1. Take care of yourself. Basically, eat food, and preferably not a double quarter pounder with cheese from McDonald's on a daily basis. No, I'm not telling you to adopt a vegetarian diet and give up root beer. Just make sure you shove fruits and vegetables in there between the root beer and chicken wings.

2. Sleep. Despite what anybody tells you, sleep is not illegal in college or higher education. In fact, if you want to survive college and not end up in the hospital for sleep deprivation (it can happen), you'll make time.

3. Relationships. Make time for family, friends, and significant others. Without them, you'll start talking to yourself in the library study carrels.

4. Socialize. Join clubs. Attend LCC events. You may even win a cool prize for attending!

5. Exercise! Yoga class or a simple 15 minute walk will help you clear your mind and regain focus.

Positive Thinking

"Whether you think you can, or you think you can't–you're right."

The quote above is from Henry Ford. It summarizes a very important message we have for you. **You create your reality.** Seriously. you make your own choices. You can choose to fail or you can choose to succeed. You can choose to study actively or you can choose to update your Facebook status. You can choose to read in the library or you can choose to read in bed. You can choose to go to class or you can choose to sleep in. You can choose to think you can or you can choose to think you can't. You get the point.

Consider this thought:

"I am no good at math. I am not cut out for this statistics class. Hopefully I at least get a C to pass."

How do you think this person will do in the course? Now consider a different thought:

"I am ready to start anew with this math class. I will keep up, seek out the help I need, and do my very best."

How do you think this student will do in the course?

The first thought sets the student up for failure and the student set the bar quite low. The second person acknowledges the past, yet has a positive outlook on what is to come in the class. Remember that your thoughts influence your attitude and outlook. And when you go into class or sit down to study with a good attitude, the experience is more enjoyable. When you enjoy what you are doing, you don't mind doing it. Now don't you want to get to the point where you enjoy studying? It is possible and it starts with your thoughts.

Once you consciously think you will succeed, set your goals, and think and act like a student ready to learn. But what about those self-doubts? Maybe you never were that great in school, or maybe you are just too hard on yourself. You can change the way you think about yourself. It takes a little practice, self-awareness and dedication. *Here are some pointers on how to change from negative thinking to positive thinking.*

- This takes practice. Start slowly. It may even help you to write down the self-defeating thoughts to gain awareness.

- Whenever you think a negative thought about yourself (your skills, progress, even appearance) immediately think of a stop sign. Stop the thought and REPLACE it with a positive thought immediately.

- Pay attention to what you verbalize about yourself as well.

Try It! How about for the next exam, you pay conscious attention to what you are telling yourself while in class, while studying and while taking the exam? Be sure to replace the negative thoughts with positive thoughts.

Discussion: Test Taking

Whenever it is a test day, I enter the class feeling confident. However, all of my classmates are frantically comparing notes and asking about terms I did not study. It really freaks me out and I lose all of my confidence. Is there any avoiding this?

– Sheila

Sometimes when I get the test in my hand, I get a little dizzy and tend to "blank out." I feel like I forgot everything I studied the night before. What am I doing wrong?

– Ricky

A few friends of mine share answers from the exam in a number of ways that I am not comfortable disclosing. They try to include me in their "answer ring" but I am hesitant. Is it worth the risk?

– Tony

Time waits for no Man

"We always think we have more time than we do"
—anonymous

There are several obstacles when it comes to time management. Many college students have to learn to balance a full course load with work and/or family. Even students that live at home and don't work can struggle with time management. Why? Not scheduling study time!

© RetroClipArt, 2012. Used under license from Shutterstock, Inc.

Who hasn't pulled an all-nighter or waited until the very last minute to start on a project? Life happens, but you need to have a plan. When friends suggest that you pay a visit to the local Starbucks, be sure that you get your studying, reading, and homework done first. You will want to convince yourself that you will get your work done in the evening once you get home. But who wants to read about the laws of physics and solve equations late at night after the basketball game or concert?

When entering college, you may not realize the little things you need on your way to success. One thing that is commonly overlooked by students is a datebook or calendar. Tracking your life is important when in college. You will have many due dates for various assignments, work, or other outside activities you're involved in. Don't let all of that overwhelm you. When you have a thousand things running through your brain, it's easy to forget things if you haven't written them down. So, PUT IT ON PAPER! Once you have written everything you need to do on a calendar . . .

1. You **will be less stressed** now that you have written everything down and can physically see what it is you need to accomplish.

2. **You have more time** to finish a future project or study for exams.

From *Engage the College Experience: How to Excel in the Classroom & Beyond* by Claudia Lilie and Christine Vodicka. Copyright © 2012 by Kendall Hunt Publishing Company. Reprinted by permission.

3. You have less to do than you think. Since your brain is a little scattered you might be over-thinking. You're most likely assuming you have more work to do than what is actually in front of you.

Follow These Rules and Rule School!

Rule #1: Avoid procrastinating at all costs. Just because nothing may be due this week or next week does not mean it's time for a two week party. Starting on projects well before they are due gives you more time to perfect the final product. This leads to better grades.

Rule #2: Break larger goals into smaller ones. Wait, this is not the goal setting chapter! Well, after you break down the large goals, do some *backwards planning*. Work backwards and schedule the goals into your planner.

Rule #3: Use a schedule! Whether you use a day planner, the templates in this book, or your phone, set a schedule! Determine where your open hours are and schedule study sessions within this time. Use an alarm/timer on your phone to keep you focused and on track.

Rule #4: Take advantage of any "found time." The time spent waiting for the bus, standing in line for the new Xbox game, or waiting in the doctor's office can all add up! Use a study log to track your study time and better understand your habits.

© RetroClipArt, 2012. Used under license from Shutterstock, Inc.

168 Hours

Did you know that there are 168 hours in one week? The 168 hours tracker on the next page allows you to see how you REALLY spend your time. Perhaps you think you study every night for hours, but it is actually just 30 minutes per night. Ouch.

Starting with tomorrow morning, begin to track when you wake up, when you are in class, when you commute, when you shop, when you go online, when you study, etc. You may be surprised at the patterns you see at the end of one week.

Take this activity a step further by highlighting different activities with different color highlighters. For instance, you can highlight all of your work time in green, all of your study time in yellow, class time in orange, and so on. This will help you get a better idea of how you spend your time as well as identify any time wasters that you should cut down on.

Once you have determined the time wasters and available time slots you were not using wisely, implement some new time management strategies, such as creating a study schedule. In a few weeks or months, track your 168 hours once more. Compare the life changes and experience the benefits of knowing where all of your time goes.

168 Hours: Activity Log

Name _____

Week of _____

	Sunday	Monday	Tuesday	Wednes	Thursday	Friday	Saturday
5:00am							
6:00am							
7:00am							
8:00am							
9:00am							
10:00am							
11:00am							
12:00pm							
1:00pm							
2:00pm							

Directions: On the day you receive the time log, start tracking how you spend your time every day, hour by hour. Do this for one full week. What did you learn about yourself?

168 Hours: Activity Log

3:00pm								
4:00pm								
5:00pm								
6:00pm								
7:00pm								
8:00pm								
9:00pm								
10:00pm								
11:00pm								
12:00am								

Directions: On the day you receive the time log, start tracking how you spend your time every day, hour by hour. Do this for one full week. What did you learn about yourself?

Daily Prioritizer

Date: September 7th

	Time	Activity
Urgent ✳ Advising Appointment	7:00 - 8:00am	
	8:00 - 9:00am	BIO 200
	9:00 - 10:00am	
	10:00 - 11:00am	ASC 101
Important ✳ Finish MTH 116 H.W. ✳ Type BIO 201 lab	11:00 - 12:00pm	
	12:00 - 1:00pm	Finish MTH 116 Homework
	1:00 - 2:00pm	ENG 100
	2:00 - 3:00pm	
Ongoing	3:00 - 4:00pm	Advising Appointment
	4:00 - 5:00pm	
	5:00 - 6:00pm	WORK
	6:00 - 7:00pm	
Trivial ✳ Lunch with Friends	7:00 - 8:00pm	
	8:00 - 9:00pm	Get off early
	9:00 - 10:00pm	
	10:00 - 11:00pm	Type BIO 201 lab

Additional Notes/Reminders:

Leave for New York on Sat. morning. Start Packing tonight!!

Daily Prioritizer   10/3

	Time	Activity
Urgent * Finish FrEX work	7:00 - 8:00am	Dogsit ↓
	8:00 - 9:00am	↓
	9:00 - 10:00am	Work on FrEX
	10:00 - 11:00am	↓
Important Po Chemistry test later!	11:00 - 12:00pm	Shower
	12:00 - 1:00pm	work
	1:00 - 2:00pm	
	2:00 - 3:00pm	
Ongoing	3:00 - 4:00pm	
	4:00 - 5:00pm	
	5:00 - 6:00pm	
	6:00 - 7:00pm	↓
Trivial Movie night with mom!	7:00 - 8:00pm	Finish FrEX
	8:00 - 9:00pm	Chemistry Test Due
	9:00 - 10:00pm	↓
	10:00 - 11:00pm	

* Write Steven a letter to bootcamp

Weekly Planner

Time	Monday	Tuesday	Wednesday	Thursday	Friday	Saturday	Sunday
7:00 - 8:00							
8:00 - 9:00		BIO 200	STUDY	BIO 200		Leave for NY	
9:00 - 10:00	BIO 201				BIO SI		
10:00 - 11:00				ASC 101			
11:00 - 12:00							
12:00 - 1:00	MTH 116		MTH 116		MTH 116		
1:00 - 2:00		ENG 100		ENG 100			
2:00 - 3:00	GYM				GYM		
3:00 - 4:00							
4:00 - 5:00	STUDY	WORK	STUDY	WORK			
5:00 - 6:00							
6:00 - 7:00							
7:00 - 8:00							
8:00 - 9:00							
9:00 - 10:00							
10:00 - 11:00							

Urgent	Important	Ongoing
*BIO201 Quiz EVERY MONDAY *MTH 116 H.W. Due EVERY FRIDAY	*Family Reunion All Weekend in New York	*ENG 100 essay due at the end of September

Weekly Planner

Week of: __10/5__

Time	Monday	Tuesday	Wednesday	Thursday	Friday	Saturday	Sunday
7:00 – 8:00	S		S				
8:00 – 9:00	T U		T U				
9:00 – 10:00	U D Y	S	U D Y	S	Med.		
10:00 – 11:00	M A	T	M A	T	Term	W	
11:00 – 12:00	T H	U	T H	U	Canceled	O	
12:00 – 1:00	Lunch ↓	D	Lunch ↓	D		R	
1:00 – 2:00		Y		Y	E	k	
2:00 – 3:00	C h		C h		N G		
3:00 – 4:00	e m	W	e m	W	L	S	
4:00 – 5:00	i s t r y	O	i s t r y	O	I S	T U	
5:00 – 6:00		R		R	Finish	D	
6:00 – 7:00	H O	R	H o	k	FYEX	Y	
7:00 – 8:00	M E		m e			Chem. Test	
8:00 – 9:00	W O		W o				
9:00 – 10:00	R k		r k				
10:00 – 11:00	study		study				

Urgent	Important		Ongoing
Study after classes.	* Finish FYEX by Sat. Mon/Wed Finish Math Hw		

MONTH OF: SEPTEMBER

Sunday	Monday	Tuesday	Wednesday	Thursday	Friday	Saturday
					1 ★ MTH H.W. 1	2
3	4 [BIO 201]	5	6	7 Advising Appointment 3pm	8 ★ MTH H.W. 2	9 Family Reunion in New York
10	11 [BIO 201]	12	13 {MTH}	14 ★ ASC Presentation	15 ★ MTH H.W. 3	16
17	18 [BIO 201]	19 [BIO 201]	20	21 {BIO 201}	22 ★ MTH H.W. 4	23
24	25 [BIO 201]	26	27	28 ★ Eng Essay	29 ★ MTH H.W. 5	30 Enjoy Today

KEY:

{ } EXAM   [ ] QUIZ   ★ DUE DATES

MONTH OF: __October__

Sunday	Monday	Tuesday	Wednesday	Thursday	Friday	Saturday
(crossed out)	(crossed out)	(crossed out)	(crossed out)	Work 3-7	English Essay *	Work 2-7 / FYEX / Chem Test
Church / Study Day	Algebra HW	Work 3-7	Algebra HW	Work 3-7	Pay Day / Med Term (review)	Work 10am-5pm / FYEX / Chem Test
Church / Study Day	Algebra HW / FYEX meeting 9:00am	Work 3-7	Algebra HW	Work 3-7	Med Term Test	Work 11am-7pm / FYEX / Chem Test
Church / Study Day	Algebra HW	Work 3-7	Algebra HW	Work 3-7	Pay Day / Med Term midterm	Work 2-7
Church / Study Day	Algebra HW	Work 3-7	Algebra HW	Work 3-7	Med Term Test	Work 2-7

PROJECT PLANNER

Name of Project/Assignment: Compare/Contrast Essay

Course: English IIII

Due Date: October 9th

Goal Grade: A+

STEP ONE: Describe the assignment. How many pages, how many points, what is expected?

I have to compare/contrast two different objects. It has to be a minimum of 3¼ pages long. It is graded on an A, B, C, D or F scale. No specific grade (EX: 95%)

STEP TWO: Determine the tasks you need to compete for the assignment. Use this checklist as a guide.

- ☒ Conduct research
- ○ Talk to the professor
- ☒ Meet with a tutor
- ○ Read the material
- ○ Form study group

- ☒ Write a draft
- ☒ Write a revision
- ☒ Write a final copy
- ○ Create study guide
- ○ Study
- ○ Other:_____

STEP THREE: Assign each task a due date to keep you on track.

Task	Date to complete by
Conduct Research	9/5
Write a draft	9/6
Write a revision	9/7
Write a Final Copy	9/8
Meet w/ a tutor before class to Check Essay	9/9

Study Log

At the beginning of the semester, a professor usually informs you how many study hours you should spend for that specific class. If it isn't given to you in the syllabus, ask the professor and write it down. You have a busy schedule, so are you really putting in the proper amount of study time for each class? Many students think they are, but after they have documented their study hours, realize it's not nearly enough.

Use the study log to document your study hours. Write down the days, class, and how long you studied for each week. You can block out time frames when you have a big chunk of time you can put into studying as well. Remember to take breaks during times like those (refer to example) so you don't overwhelm yourself. At the end of the week, add up your hours and find out if you have been slacking or are right on schedule.

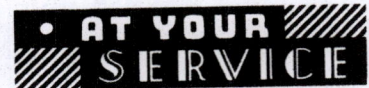

STUDY LOG

Week of: ___September 18th___

Date	Subject(s)	Start Time	End Time	Total Time
9/18	BIO 200/201	4 PM	6 PM	2 hrs
	MTH 116	7 PM	8 PM	1 hr
9/19	ENG 100 (read)	10 AM	11 AM	1 hr
	BIO 200	11 PM	1 AM	2 hrs
9/20	MTH 116	10 AM	11 AM	1 hr
	BIO 201	11 AM	12 AM	1 hr
	BIO 200	4 PM	9 PM	5 hrs
	* 30min Break every hour *			
9/22	ENG 100 (Essay)	5 PM	7 PM	2 hrs

Grand Total: ___15 hrs___

STUDY LOG

Week of: _____

Date	Subject(s)	Start Time	End Time	Total Time

Grand Total: _____

STUDY LOG

Week of: _____

Date	Subject(s)	Start Time	End Time	Total Time

Grand Total: _____

Discussion: Time Management

> I am a wife and mother to a two-year-old son. I'm also taking care of my sick father. On top of that I work part-time. I've just returned to school to finish my Bachelors. How do I make "me" time to reduce the stress levels?
>
> – Karen

> My grandmother recently died and my parents announced they are splitting. I am so overwhelmed I have been falling behind on homework assignments and my test grades reflect it. Where can I get help managing the stress and making time for school in my hectic life?
>
> – Daniel

> Between working full time, classes, homework, and studying, I'm lucky if I get three hours of sleep a night. It's really starting to take its toll on my health. What can I do to make more time for sleep in my life?
>
> – Jennifer

Ready, Set, Read

7

Active Reading

"You cannot open a book without learning something."
—Confucius

As college students you encounter reading in every course you take. Many of you are shocked by the homework expectations. In the first four weeks of a term, it is not unusual for professors to assign 70 pages of reading each time the class meets. College level courses typically have two to four exams

© RetroClipArt, 2012. Used under license from Shutterstock, Inc.

which will be based on 200 to 400 pages of reading in addition to lecture material. It is easy to see how study time begins to add up.

Fellow students have asked . . .

"I have read for three hours straight and cannot remember a thing. What should I do?"

You are not alone. Many students put in the time required, diligently read the assigned chapters, and understand the author's points. Yet when asked to recall information from the reading, they cannot provide specific details.

You need to be an active reader. Do something with the information you read. Attending lecture or looking at words on a written page does not create meaning. Take notes, look for the main idea and define vocabulary. While reading, reflect on what was written and then try to apply the concepts to your life. Make the information meaningful to you—especially if it does not seem to apply

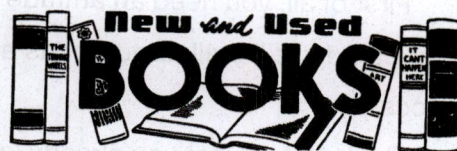

From *Engage the College Experience: How to Excel in the Classroom & Beyond* by Claudia Lilie and Christine Vodicka. Copyright © 2012 by Kendall Hunt Publishing Company. Reprinted by permission.

to your life. Information that is not used is more likely to be forgotten as soon as you close the book. To truly understand the meaning of what you are reading, you need to interact with what is read.

"I will never finish this!"

So you have eight chapters to read and it is two nights before the exam. Don't panic. Make a plan instead.

1. Determine exactly how many pages you will be reading. How long will this take you to read and comprehend the material?

2. Break the reading up into smaller time slots. Take short 5–10 minute breaks in between each section. Review what you read before the break and then begin the new section.

3. Review pictures and information in the margins.

4. Skim through the information discussed in class, slowing down to cover confusing topics.

5. Carefully read new material not covered in class, using active reading strategies.

6. Create one or two questions for each section that might be on the test.

"I just read the chapter and do not understand anything I read. Buying the book was a waste of money; I do not even read it anymore."

First of all, you need an attitude change. Tell yourself, "I am going to read this and remember it." You can do it; it's all about focus and positive thinking. If you say you cannot do it, you will never succeed.

Think about what you already know by using a KWL map (Know, Wonder, Learn) for assistance. In the left column (**K**now), write the facts you know about the topic. In the middle column (**W**onder), answer the question, "What do I want to know about this topic," or write questions you want to answer while you read. Finally, when you have completed a section (not the entire chapter), write down the answers to your questions (**L**earned). See the example started below.

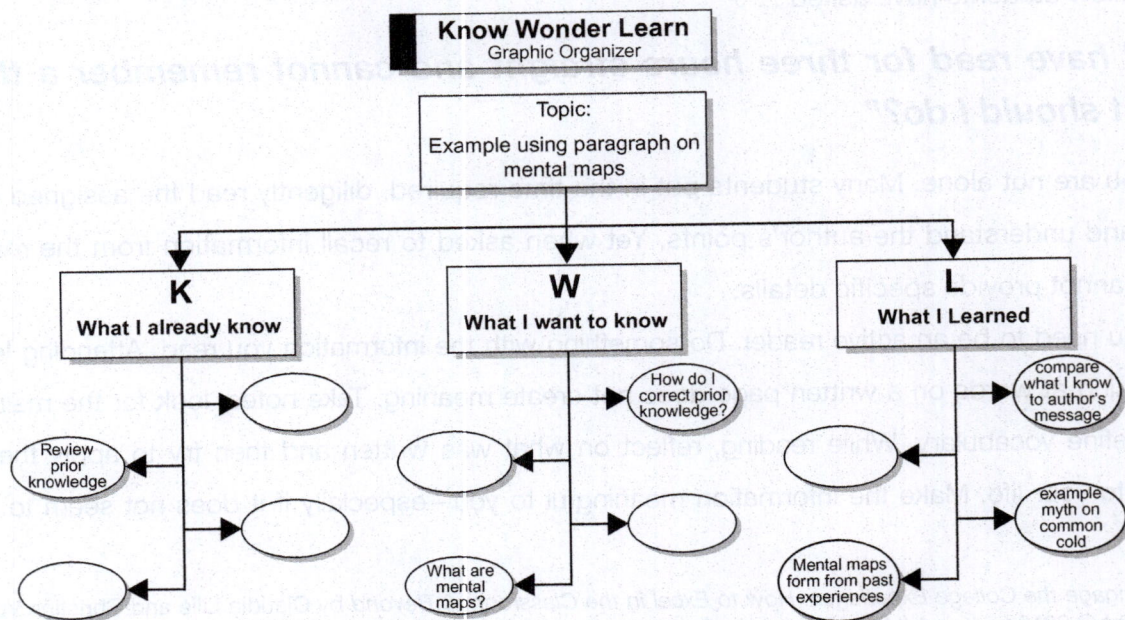

Know Wonder Learn
Graphic Organizer

Topic:
Example using paragraph on mental maps

K — What I already know

W — What I want to know

L — What I Learned

Review prior knowledge

How do I correct prior knowledge?

What are mental maps?

compare what I know to author's message

example myth on common cold

Mental maps form from past experiences

If you are still struggling: SEEK OUT HELP! Contact your professor and ask specific questions, go to TASC and sign up for tutoring, or study with a friend who is willing to help you understand the material. Do not give up.

Stress: the way your mind and body reacts to physical, psychological, and/or emotional demands.

>**Eustress:** good stress; stress that will motivate one to complete tasks.

>**Distress:** negative stress; often interferes with getting tasks completed.

Causes of Stress

Expectations we place on ourselves

Expectations of others

Our physical environment (noise, weather, seasons changing)

Our internal environment (academic pressure, frustration, decision making)

Relaxation: an activity or recreation that provides relief, diversion, and/or entertainment.

Overview of Relaxation

-Many individuals have a limited view of what it means to be relaxed

-Relaxation does not mean simply letting your shoulders down and taking a deep breath

-Relaxation means no excess tension, a condition of physiological and psychological balance and efficiency

Benefits of Relaxation

-Enhances focus, attention, and concentration

-Decreases heart rate

-Decreases blood pressure

-Oxygen delivery is more efficient

-Strengthens the immune system

Relaxation/Stress-Reducing Techniques

Deep breathing

Visualization

Exercise

Massage therapy

Entertainment/laughter

Healthy diet

Adequate sleep

Stress-Related Illnesses

Digestive problems

Upset stomach

Heartburn

Constipation

Diarrhea

Ulcers

Headaches/migraines

High blood pressure/heart attack/stroke

Muscle/joint pain

Cold/flu

Respiratory/sinus infections

Negative Responses to Stress

Drugs

Alcohol

Depression

Suicide

Unhealthy/risky sexual behavior

Past Experiences Form Your Mental Map

Everyone has their own mental map of the world. Your past experiences create your knowledge, or what you know about the subjects. When you read, you compare what the author is saying to your own mental map. What you take away from the text can be totally different from your best friend. There are also times when you need to change your perception of the topic to understand what the author is trying to tell you. If your prior perception is not altered, you will have trouble constructing meaning using the new information. To be successful at reading, you need to use the correct prior knowledge and the necessary processing strategies to comprehend the author's message. Only you can comprehend and use the information. Your friend cannot do it for you. This is why you may have trouble reading a nuclear fusion book while your friend breezes through it.

To understand how important your mental map is to reading try the exercise below.

1. Read the following passage. As you read it, examine what your brain is doing to understand it, and decide upon a title for the passage.

   Title _____

   Consider using different types for different populations and environments. You can buy them at a specialty shop or find them on your own. Some people prefer the fake ones, but they don't always work as well. They seem to have a sixth sense and can tell when it isn't real. In addition, they can often smell you on it and this alerts them to stay away. Try using gloves when you handle them. However, when there is a dense population it doesn't seem to matter as much. Just make sure it looks alive when it moves. Depending on the size, you may need to cut it into pieces and thread it through the center of each piece, letting parts of them dangle from the sides. You can also use several whole pieces depending on the size of your equipment. If you use a big one, thread the entire segment, letting the end hang off. Whatever the size, make sure it is secure.

2. What was your brain doing while you were reading?

3. Why did you find it hard to grasp? What is missing that caused you to have trouble understanding the author's message?

4. What did you do to help yourself construct meaning? What fix-it strategies did you try to use to help you understand?

Did you encounter this while reading?

As I read the passage, I was able to decode the words but not understand the sentence. When I tried to compare my previous knowledge on the subject to the author's message, something was wrong. I noticed the pronouns in the passage were not clear, which made reading the passage confusing. I struggled to find meaning and finally gave up. The strategies I tried did not work and I decided I did not need to know the information.

What if you knew that the passage was about fishing worms? Would this information help you understand the author's message? Why?

5. Reread the passage, it should be easier to read this time!

The second time through the paragraph, you were able to draw on your own mental map of how to bait a fishing hook using worms. Even if you have never fished, your brain had some picture of how this process was to occur. This prior picture and the new information contained in the passage allowed you to create a new mental map. This, in the end, allowed you to actively read what the author was telling you.

Highlight Much?

Ever look over your text book and realize that you highlighted all but two words on a page? Are your markers running as dry as dust? Do you wish you were color blind and could not work with bright colors anymore? If any of these questions apply to you or if you are looking for ideas about effective underlining and highlighting skills while studying, there are tips to proactively change the way you mark and distinguish the pertinent information of class material.

- ✔ **Know your limit!** Setting a cap on how much you plan on distinguishing information that you want to reference for later may help avoid the highlighting crazies. Just like with summarizing or paraphrasing, there are reasons why condensing material is friendly to your brain and your ability to remember key concepts. Some study experts (didn't even know there was such a thing) recommend limiting your markings to once or twice per paragraph. This is because reading is an active learning process and highlighting is a visual and physical cue to your brain to recognize the importance of what you marked.

- ✔ **The only time you don't have to mark the thesis!** Although detecting the author's thesis is essential in determining the author's main idea, you do not automatically mark it for this reason. Often the thesis is not as useful as the real-world examples the text gives. These application phrases or sentences show rather than tell.

- ✔ **Vary your markings:** Stripes of color aren't the only visuals you may put down on paper! Try developing your own secret code of organizing key ideas by indicating what type of information you mean to record. For example, you may want to underline phrases, box key words, or put asterisks next to a larger section you want to identify.

- ✔ **Your chance to edit:** Before you think "wait that is not my job" consider the goal of editing: to figuratively weed out and dig up the core ideas the author is communicating. This will help you get to the point and be selective while reading, allowing you to have a deeper and more thorough understanding of the important concepts.

- ✔ **Try other modes of transportation:** Think about expanding your means of marking by using supplies other than highlighters to allow for more variety (and ease for your eyes).

Annotating in five easy steps

Sometimes you have no prior knowledge on a subject or your prior mental map is not totally correct. An example of this would be the first time you read a history book. The events, dates, and times can become confusing and difficult to sort out; however, if you just move on, the information would be lost. Again, you need to interact with the information by annotating your textbook. Yes, this means writing in the textbook. To truly understand new concepts, you need to mark up the textbook. The strategy contains five steps that, with practice, will become a natural habit.

Annotating in five easy steps

1. Find short phrases that succinctly express the main idea. Draw a box around it and write Main Idea.

2. Find brief definitions. Circle the terms, underline the definition, and write "DEF" in the margin.

3. Write ex (for example) in the margins next to any example or illustration.

4. Put a ? next to things you do not understand.

5. Put an ! next to things you think are important.

You do not always have to do all the above. It will depend on what you are reading. In four to six weeks of continued use, you will annotate without thinking about the steps. Give it some time and try it out.

Without review, annotating is a waste of time. After the completion of reading the page, chapter or passage, do not forget to complete this last step. Imagine you will be tested on this passage. Write two test questions based on the passage. Find the answer to the questions using the annotations you made while reading.

Let's try this out on the passage below.

Read the paragraph from Michael Pollan's book *In Defense of Food* (pages 70–72). The passage discusses how to study the impact of diet on health.

As you read, mark the passage using the five steps for annotating.

"*But if confounding factors of lifestyle bedevil epidemiological comparisons of different populations, the supposedly more rigorous studies of large American populations suffer from their own arguably even more disabling flaws. In ascending order of supposed reliability, nutrition researchers have three main methods for studying the impact of diet on health: the case-control study, the cohort study, and the intervention trail. All three are seriously flawed in different ways.*

In the case-control study, researchers attempt to determine the diet of a subject who has been diagnosed with a chronic disease in order to uncover its cause. One problem is that when people get sick they may change the way they eat, so the diet they report may not be the diet responsible for their illness. Another problem is that the patients will typically report eating large amounts of whatever the evil nutrient of the moment is....

...Long-term observational studies of cohort groups such as the Nurses' Health Study represent a big setup in the reliability from the case-control study. For one thing the studies are prospective rather than retrospective. They begin tracking subjects before they become ill."

Michael Pollan. 2008. *In Defense of Food: An Eater's Manifesto.* (Kindle Location 914). Penguin Group. Kindle Edition.

Imagine you are in a nutrition class. What two questions might be on the test based on the passage?

1.

2.

How does yours compare to the one below?

> "But if confounding factors of lifestyle bedevil epidemiological comparisons of different populations, the supposedly more rigorous studies of large American populations suffer from their own arguably even more disabling flaws. In ascending order of supposed reliability, nutrition researchers have three main methods for studying the impact of diet on health: the case-control study, the cohort study, and the intervention trail. All three are seriously flawed in different ways.
>
> **Main Idea**
>
> In the case-control study, researchers attempt to determine the diet of a subject who has been diagnosed with a chronic disease in order to uncover its cause. One problem is that when people get sick they may change the way they eat, so the diet they report may not be the diet responsible for their illness. Another problem is that the patients will typically report eating large amounts of whatever the evil nutrient of the moment is...
>
> **!**
>
> ...Long-term observational studies of cohort groups such as the Nurses' Health Study represent a big setup in the reliability from the case-control study. For one thing the studies are prospective rather than retrospective. They begin tracking subjects before they become ill.
>
> **EX**

Imagine you are taking a nutrition class. What two questions might be on the test based on the passage?

1. Discuss the flaws of the case-control study and its impact on the participants diet and health.

2. Which of the studies is the most reliable? Why?

Concept Mapping

Think You're a "Visual Learner"?

If so, this is the PERFECT study tool for you! Concepts maps are a FUN way to study. When you make studying fun, you will retain the information you need to know. Maps give you an opportunity to connect concepts in your own way by using colors or drawing pictures in an organized fashion. REMEMBER: this is a study tool for YOU so you can be as creative as you want!

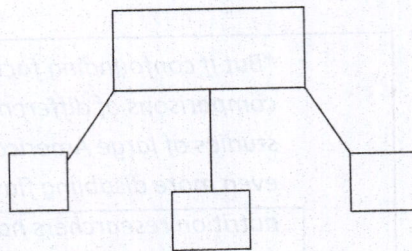

*BONUS of CONCEPT MAPPING: becoming an active learner!

What you will need:

- ➤ Blank, white or color paper
- ➤ Color pencils, pens or markers
- ➤ Textbook
- ➤ Lecture notes

Guidelines For Creating a Concept Map

1. Take out your textbook or lecture notes and look for bold words or phrases.

2. Pull out ALL the information that revolves around that key word or phrase.

3. Get your blank paper and put the word or phrase in a box at the top. This will be your main idea for your concept map.

4. Take the additional information and start branching off of your main idea.

5. When you have completed your concept map, you should be able to look at it and explain why the boxes or pictures connect in the way that you have created.

Student Example A

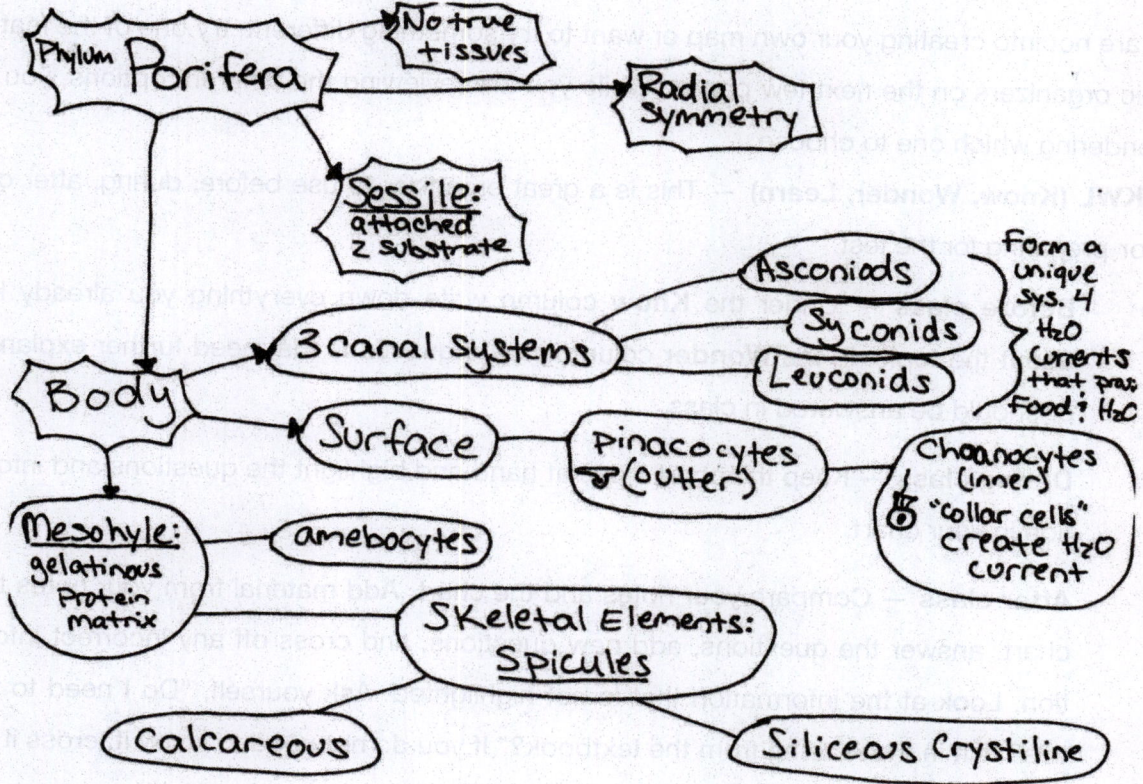

Student Example B

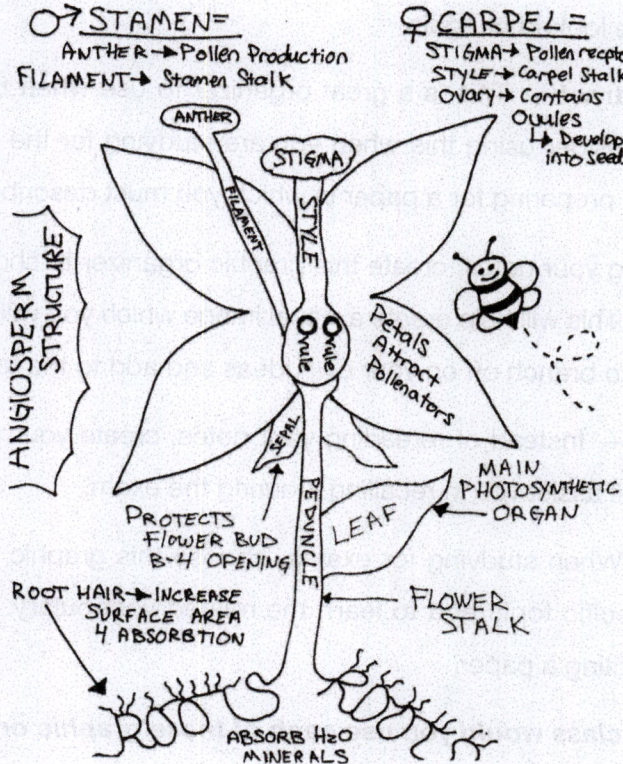

Graphic Organizers

If you are not into creating your own map or want to try something different, try one of the featured graphic organizers on the next few pages. While you are reviewing the different options, you may be wondering which one to choose.

1. **KWL (Know, Wonder, Learn)** — This is a great organizer to use before, during, after class, or preparing for the test.

    Before class — Under the **Know** column write down everything you already know about the topic. In the **Wonder** column create questions that need further explanation or should be answered in class.

    During class — Keep the chart close at hand and highlight the questions and information in your chart.

    After class — Compare your notes and the chart. Add material from your notes to the chart, answer the questions, add new questions, and cross off any incorrect information. Look at the information that is not highlighted. Ask yourself, "Do I need to know this? Is it in the reading from the textbook?" If you do not need to know it, cross it off.

    Preparing for a test — Using a blank form, fill in all the columns with what you learned about the topic. Any questions that cannot be answered or topics with only minor details need to be looked at again.

2. **Compare and Contrast** — This is a great organizer to use when first sorting out unfamiliar information. Also consider using this when you are studying for the exam to test your knowledge; or use it when preparing for a paper in which you must describe both sides.

3. **Main Ideas** — Using your notes, create this graphic organizer to show the important information about the topic. This will help create a visual image which you will recall in your mind during the exam. Feel free to branch off on your own ideas and add to the template.

4. **Study Guide Map** — Instead of rereading your notes, create your own study guide. Actively using information will assist you in recalling it during the exam.

5. **Break it Down** — When studying for exams, choose this graphic organizer to expand your knowledge of a specific topic and to learn the related vocabulary. Another use is to narrow your topic before writing a paper.

In which class would you use each of these graphic organizers?

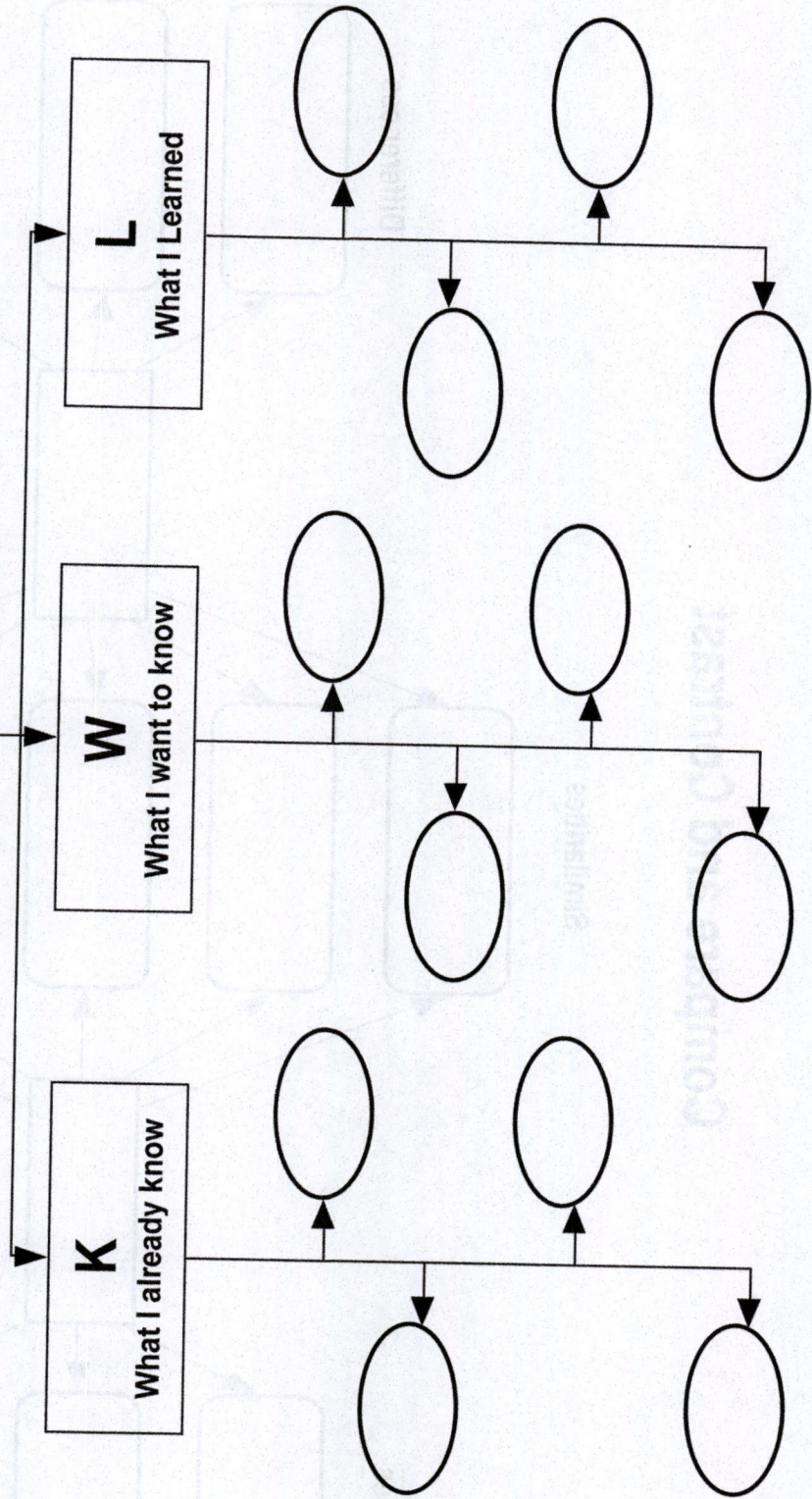

Know Wonder Learn
Graphic Organizer

Topic:

K
What I already know

W
What I want to know

L
What I Learned

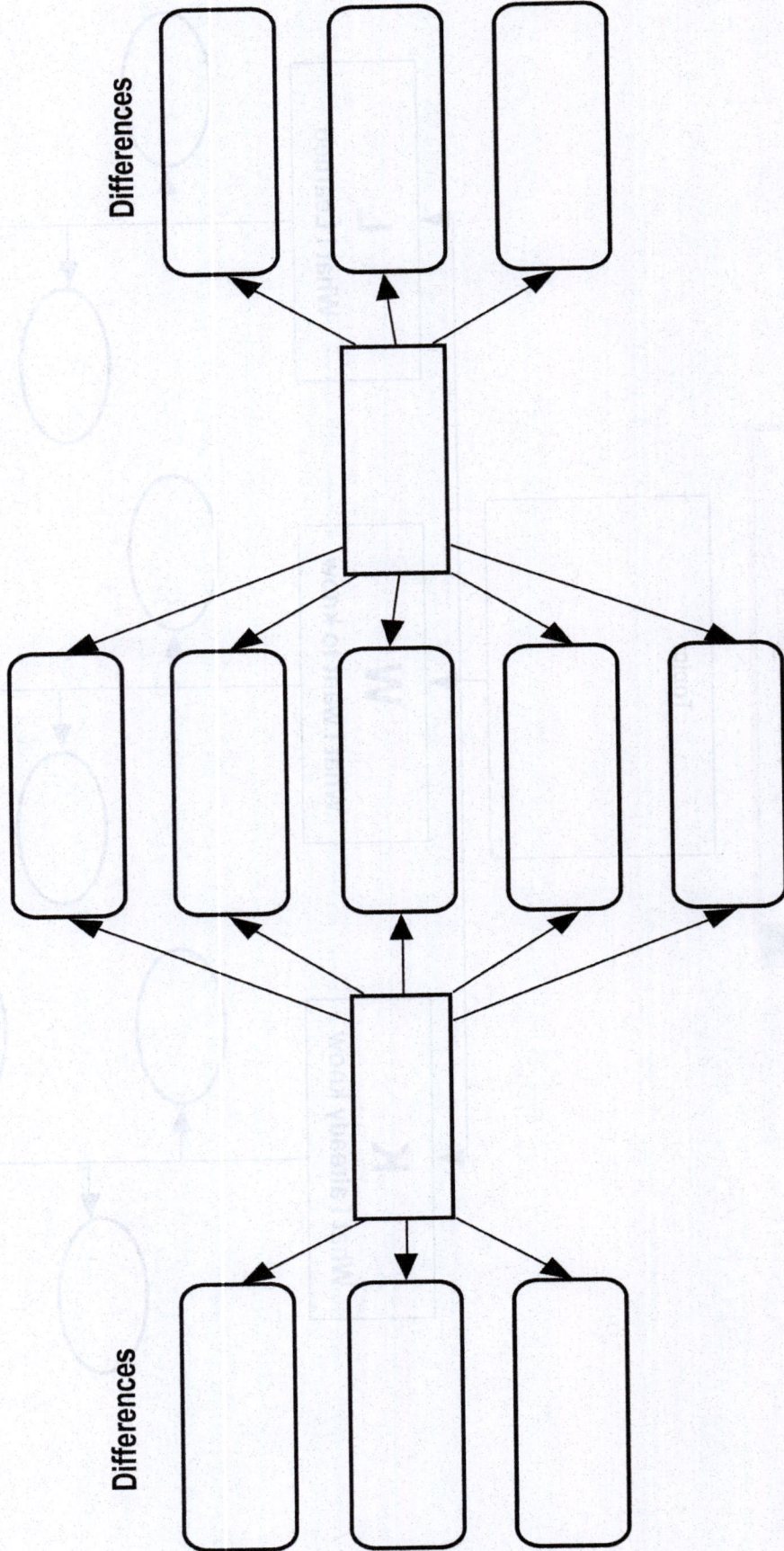

Compare and Contrast

Differences

Similarities

Differences

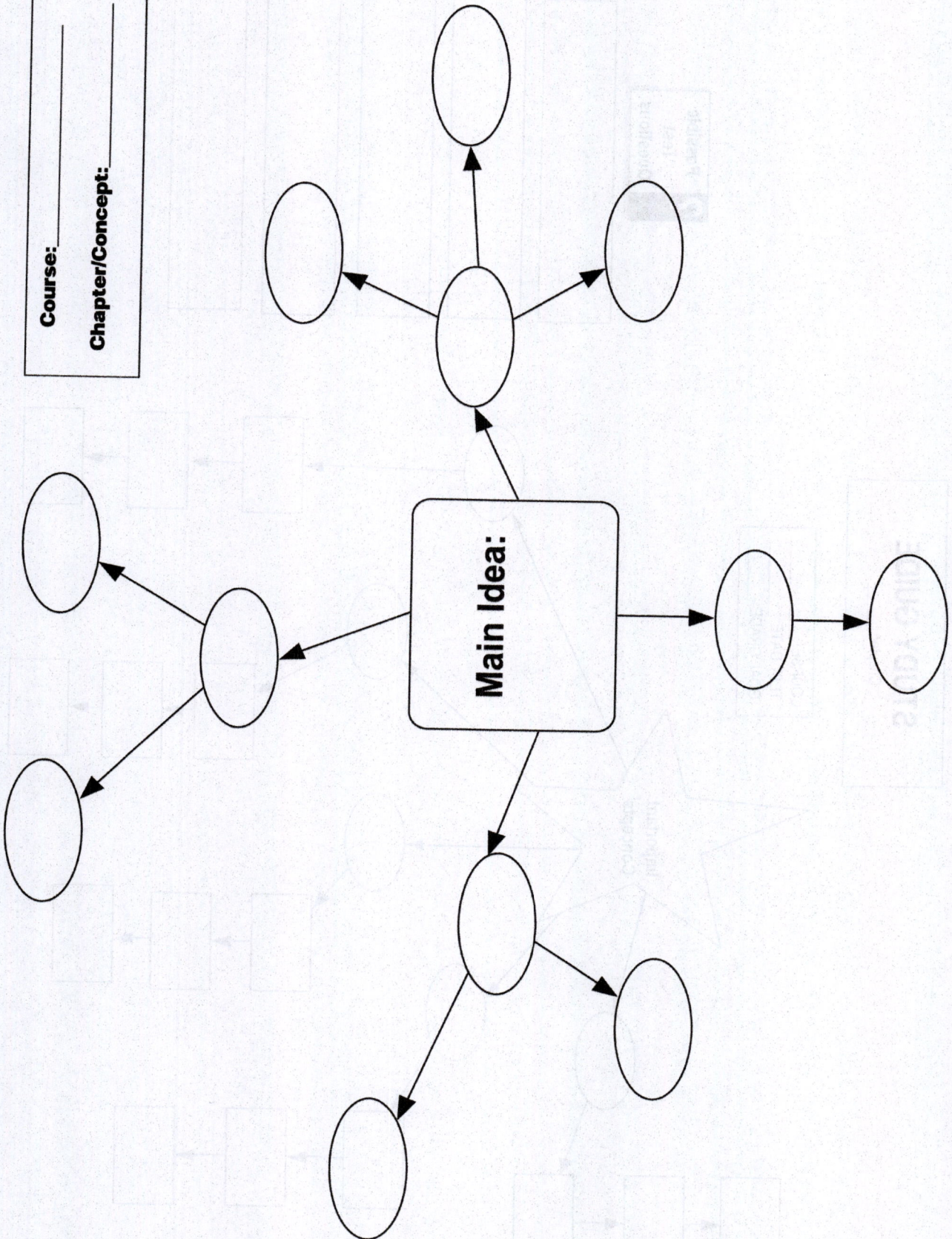

Course: _____

Chapter/Concept: _____

Main Idea:

STUDY GUIDE

Chapter: _____

COURSE: _____
TEST DATE: _____
GOAL GRADE: _____

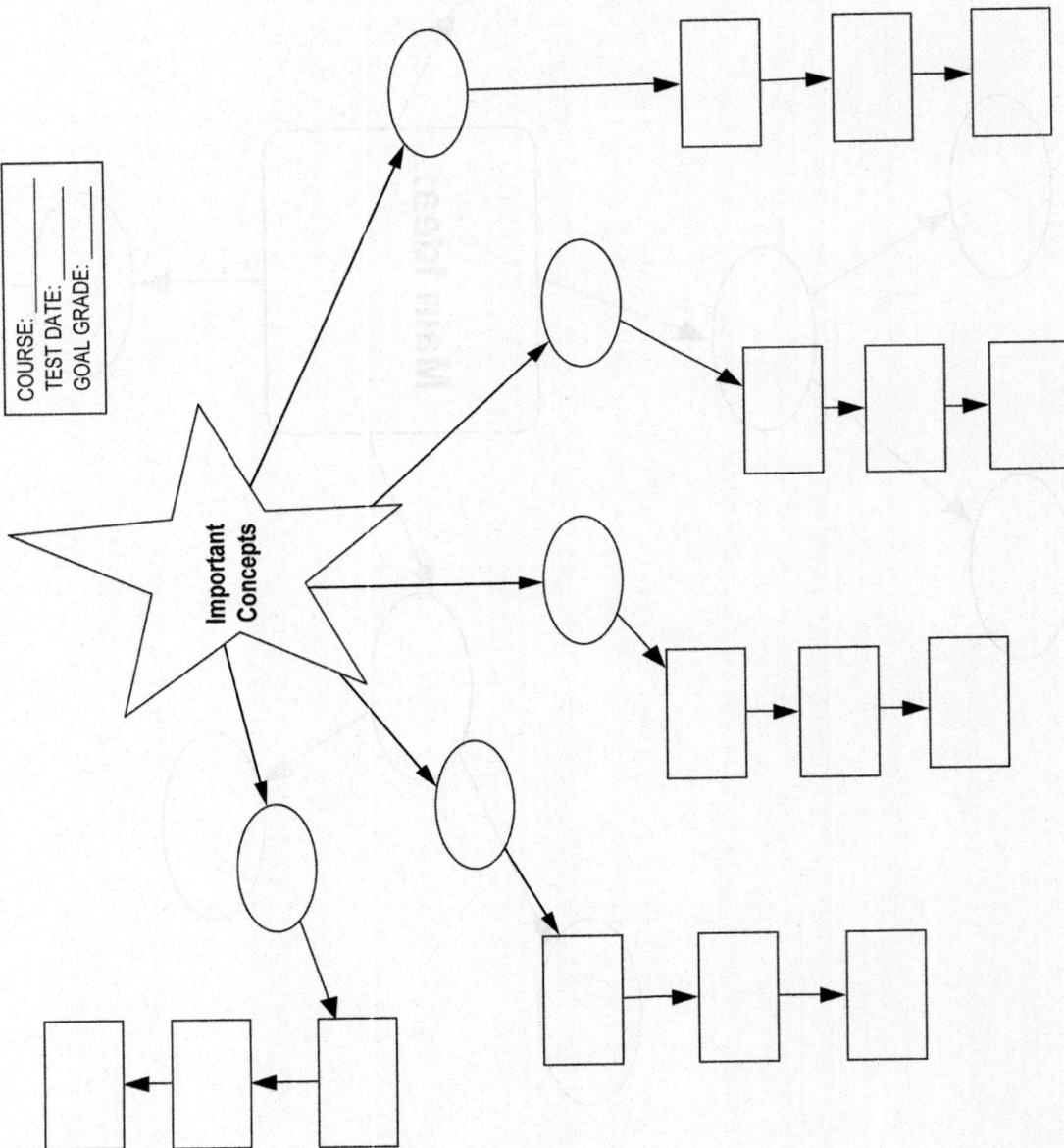

Possible Test Questions

?

Important Concepts

Break it Down

Take tough concepts and make them more comprehendible with this graphic organizer!

Discuss and List Five Important Concepts
1.   2.   3.   4.   5.
Choose One Concept and Relate Four Ideas
1.   2.   3.   4.
Choose and Define Three New Words
1.   2.   3.
In Your own Words Discuss Two Concepts or Ideas You Already Knew
1.   2.
Write One Question You Still Have
1.

Discussion: Active Reading

I disagree with the author's view. It makes reading this book really hard. I also think my professor doesn't value my comments if they do not agree with hers. Help!

– Taylor

I find marking the important information difficult using my iPad. Are there any features or shortcuts that would help me?

– Anthony

I was told by the bookstore that I can write in my textbooks and still return them as long as it is in pencil and not too excessive. Knowing this, how should I proceed marking my textbook?

– Damian

Learn to Earn

Organization, Studying, and Note-Taking

"When reviewing your notes before an exam, the most important will be illegible."
—Murphy's Law

Get Organized!

Perhaps you went shopping for school supplies prior to the semester. What items did you buy? The reason we ask is that we recommend a "tool kit." Having the right materials on hand will make your studying experience more effective, and quite possibly more enjoyable.

© RetroClipArt, 2012. Used under license from Shutterstock, Inc.

In fact, by having a variety of supplies at your fingertips, you can take your learning to the next level. Here are some examples of going above and beyond in the name of success:

- Use write-on tabs to tab your textbook chapters for easy reference.
- Use sticky notes to add questions and summaries to the textbook chapters (especially if you are hesitant to write in your book).
- Use two different color pens as a coding system. For instance, use a blue or black pen to take notes in class and use a red pen to add textbook notes to your lecture notes.
- Keep a two inch binder for each of your classes. Invest in a three hole punch and some tab dividers. Label each of your sections with headings such as:
  - Syllabus, class notes, homework, tests/quizzes, study guides, maps, research, papers, etc.

Tool Kit Shopping List

In addition to textbooks, the following are recommended for success . . .

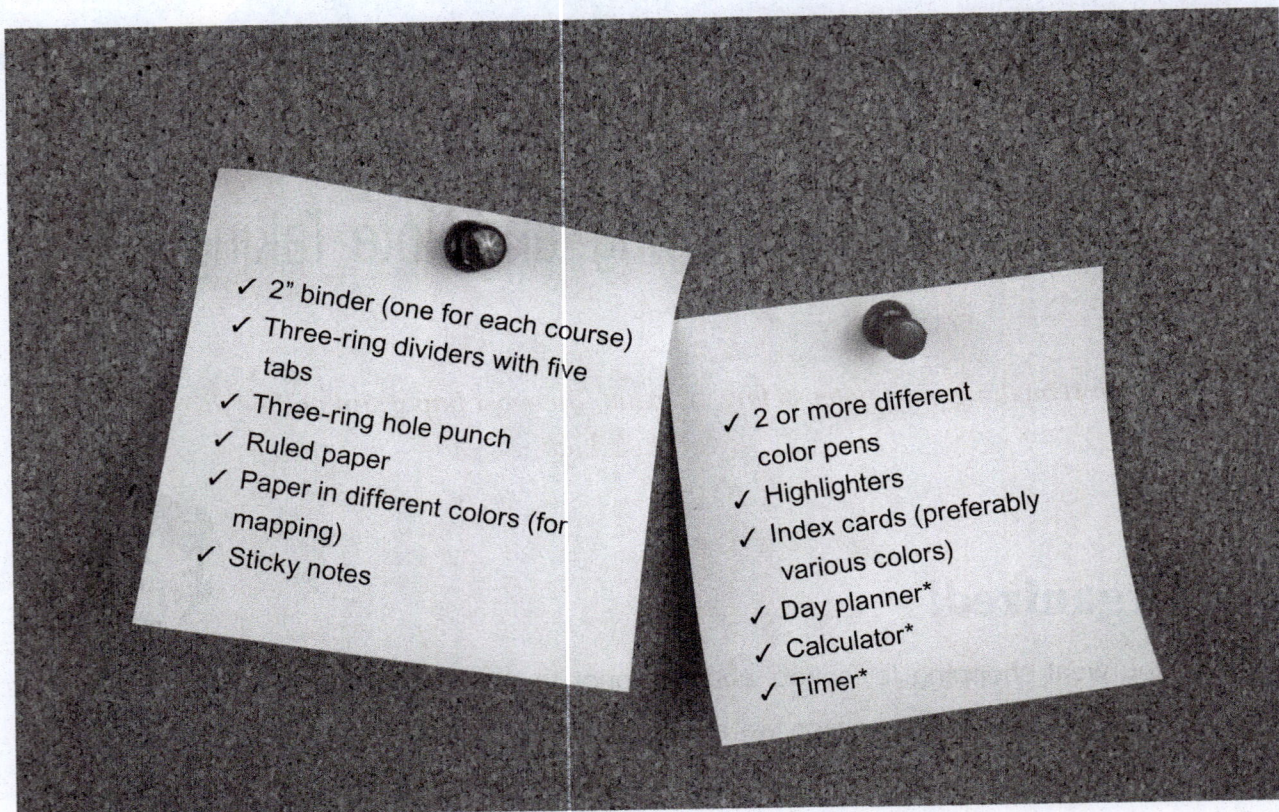

- ✓ 2" binder (one for each course)
- ✓ Three-ring dividers with five tabs
- ✓ Three-ring hole punch
- ✓ Ruled paper
- ✓ Paper in different colors (for mapping)
- ✓ Sticky notes

- ✓ 2 or more different color pens
- ✓ Highlighters
- ✓ Index cards (preferably various colors)
- ✓ Day planner*
- ✓ Calculator*
- ✓ Timer*

© tkemot, 2014. Used under license from Shutterstock, Inc.

These items are also available in the latest technology. Feel free to use your iPad or smartphone for these items. If you are too distracted by your technology, it is then recommended that you purchase the items separately as needed.

So You Think You Can Study?

Before you sit down to study, ask yourself some quick questions first.

1. **What environment do you study best in?**

THINK!

Where do you feel you will accomplish the most work?

Do you like listening to loud music when you study?

Watching TV? Probably NOT a good spot, you'll end up watching the TV instead of studying.

Would you prefer going to a quiet coffee house?

All Images © RetroClipArt, 2012. Used under license from Shutterstock, Inc.

Is the sound level appropriate? Everyone likes different levels of background noise when they sit down to study. There are those who listen to music, go to coffee houses, or like a completely silent area. Whatever it is that you decide, remember, IT'S WHAT WORKS BEST FOR YOU! If you are finding that the study area you picked originally isn't working out because you're getting distracted, find a new location. It's never too late to try something new! Especially if the outcome of the change is beneficial to your study habits!

2. **Is it comfortable?** You want the area you're going to be in for a significant amount of time to be somewhere you feel comfortable, but not too comfortable. Don't kid yourself into thinking that lying in bed will be the perfect spot to start studying. Although it is comfortable, it's probably too comfortable. Chances are that you may fall asleep while trying to do your work.

3. **How's the lighting?** Make sure the lights are bright enough for you to see your books. If the lights are dim, you will find that you're squinting and straining your eyes, making you tired. So, find a well-lit spot. Something bright enough to keep you awake but not an area that is so bright it's blinding.

4. **Is the area uncluttered?** Make sure the area you picked is free of clutter. If you're sitting in a spot that has random items scattered around that are NOT associated with what you're studying, they will distract you. Let's be real here, you probably don't want to study so, if you have a bunch of random stuff in front of you, chances are you'll get distracted by it and won't study.

5. **Do you have all the supplies you will need?** Before you get curled up with your books, make sure you have everything you need before you get comfortable. You don't want to keep getting up to get pens, markers, etc., when you're ready to study. It will distract you and take away from study time.

Top 10 Study Tips
By: Halley Daniels, CSU Success Coach

10. Be sure to study in a quiet place where you are able to really focus and concentrate. Keep all of your study supplies (note cards, calculator, pens, paper, etc.) in the same place, so that when it comes time for you to study, you are not wasting time searching for these items.

9. Take some extra time to research or learn about new study techniques, like outlining, memory cards, concept maps, annotating. You may discover a new technique that helps you to retain information better than a previous method you had used. Also, go to the Tutoring and Academic Success Center (Main Classroom 233) to sign up with a tutor or a success coach, both of whom can help you immensely with either specific subjects or perfecting study skills.

8. Talk to your professors and become familiar with them. This will show your professors that you care about the class and your grade, and will help you out in the long run. Also, speak with your professors before tests to inquire what will be covered on exams, so that you know exactly what to study.

7. Make sure you take periodic breaks throughout your study time. Try to study for 50 minutes and then take a 10 minute break and repeat. When you take your break, try to empty your mind of studying and focus your attention elsewhere. A timer is also a great tool to use so that you do not keep glancing at the clock to know when your break is (there is probably a timer in your phone!). Also, you may want to go for a short walk or eat a snack, so you can come back to studying refreshed and ready to focus again.

6. As you study, highlight or put a star next to topics that you do not know as well as others, so that you remember to study those topics harder. This will allow you to spend more time on topics you aren't as familiar with, rather than spending equal amounts of time on all topics.

5. While you are studying, be sure to minimize distractions like the Internet, texting, talking on the phone, etc. so that you can really focus and concentrate on the material.

4. Get a study buddy from your class! A study buddy is a great person to study with because they learn the same material that you do. This can also help studying to be livelier and more engaging, which in turn could help you retain the information better.

3. Be sure to review the previous lecture's material a few minutes before your next lecture. If you do this regularly, you will be able to continuously form the connections of the topics you are learning from lecture to lecture. This will also help you be able to get a better handle on what you will be learning about during that day's lecture, so that you can understand the material better, as well as ask important questions.

2. Schedule yourself permanent study blocks or 'study halls' in your weekly schedule so that your study time does not accidentally get cut out. If you form this habit at the beginning of the semester, you will come to think of study time as an integral part of your schedule, rather than a chore. Also, having a permanent study block will ensure that you do study and not put it off.

1. Begin to study right after the test! After you take an exam, you may want to take a break from learning and studying. However, it is important to begin studying for the next exam right away so you do not lose touch from your school work, and also so you do not stop the flow of learning from topic to topic.

Learning to Learn Quick Tips

- Schedule, Schedule, Schedule!! Studying and learning involves time, and finding this time may be a challenge (especially when you are in college). Develop a time management plan by creating a weekly schedule of your classes, work schedule, and activities to help you see where you can fit in extra time devoted to learning content. Perhaps you have ten minutes waiting for the bus, 7 minutes waiting for your food to thaw, or 15 minutes waiting for your laundry to dry! These valuable times will add up and you will reap the benefits of your preparation!

- Know Yourself: Learn not only about your preferred mode of learning, but how you can incorporate your personal style and your learning. Are you a visual learner? You might want to think about using concept cards, drawing out ideas, or creating diagrams or visual organizers. Are you an auditory learner? Then you may want to 'think aloud' the important concepts in your classes with a study buddy and taking a practice test orally may be very reinforcing.

- Give me a break! That's right, give yourself the freedom to pause to give your hard-working mind a breather, rather than cramming tons of information.

Study Buddy Information Tracker

Why are Study Buddies important?

- Compare notes from class and improve your notes
- Quiz and learn from each other's strengths
- Study through discussion
- Create and share study guides
- See what you missed in class
- Increased motivation

© RetroClipArt, 2012. Used under license from Shutterstock, Inc.

Course	Student Name	Phone	Email	Best Days/Times

Guidelines for Studying with Peers / Study Groups:

1. Come prepared with textbook, notes, laptop (if needed), and questions!

2. Meet in a quiet, public place.

3. Choose your study buddies wisely!

4. Limit the number of study group members to 4 to 6.

5. Set an agenda and stay on track. A moderator or timekeeper helps.

Note-Taking 101

Just. Take. Notes. It's that simple. Do not rely on your memory to get you a good grade on the test. Oftentimes there will be weeks between tests. I don't know about you, but it is hard to remember what we ate two nights ago, let alone Newtonian physics. Do yourself a favor and take notes, whether on your laptop or in a standard wire bound notebook.

Once you have taken notes, what happens next? It is time to do something with your notes. Of course, you should read them over and review them, but that is not enough. Too often students study by "looking over" their notes. This is a form of passive learning. It is time to engage with learning.

Apply some of these helpful strategies in order to engage with your notes and enhance recall on the exam.

✔ Transfer your notes onto the Cornell note-taking template.

✔ Compare your lecture notes to your textbook and add text notes to fill in the gaps. In fact, use a different color pen for your textbook notes.

© RetroClipArt, 2012. Used under license from Shutterstock, Inc.

✔ Apply the Fold Out strategy to help you compare notes with text. You will be completing a helpful study guide in the process.

✔ Divide concepts and rewrite notes onto "concept cards." Concept cards are large 5" by 7" index cards which include the term, definition, example, page numbers, diagrams, etc.

✔ Some people prefer to type their notes after class for readability. This is a great review in itself.

While in Class: Ways to Engage

1. Sit in the front of the classroom or lecture hall.

2. Be prepared. Are there any slides you need to print? Do you have your notebook or binder and a pen (that works)?

3. As cool as your friends are, try not to sit with them or at least let them know you must refrain from banter or gabbing while you take expert notes.

4. Make eye contact with your professor. This lets the professor know you are awake and eager to learn.

5. Avoid Facebook, eBay, or any other inappropriate online material while in lecture class. If the laptop is too distracting, make the right decision and leave it in your bag or at home.

6. Be sure to turn off your cell phone. No one wants to hear your David Guetta ringtone. You are not fooling anyone if you put the phone on vibrate.

7. If your professor talks fast and you cannot keep up, consider purchasing a voice recorder. Be sure to run this by your professor.

Cornell Note-Taking

Cornell notes are a super easy way to organize your lecture notes in terms of the key words, concepts, and theories that the professor will present in class.

a. The first column can be used for key concepts or theories. Key words and concepts are those vocabulary words or theories you will encounter during the lecture. List them here.

b. The second column should be used to take notes on the professor's class lecture. Here you will have a written record of the professor's particular take on the subject matter.

c. Below both columns should be a section dedicated to summary. After each class take the time to summarize the material from the lecture and connect the dots between all of the key words, concepts, and theories that day. Don't just paraphrase!

Each professor is different and because of this, each professor does not present subject material as it is presented in your books and readings. Know their perspective! The lecture notes demand their own special strategy because it is the lecture that the professor will usually draw from most in writing tests and assignments.

Finally, remember that you can customize Cornell notes and play with the formatting. Change the headings, add more sections, or even decorate and doodle in your notes if said decorations and doodles are relevant to the material. Your goal is to learn, but in order to learn, you need to make it enjoyable for yourself. See examples starting on page 34.

Summarization Quick Tips

Did you wake up on the wrong side of the bed this morning? Do you want to learn to summarize more effectively? You may be wondering what the first events of your day have to do with summarizing, but think about it . . . you use summarizing a lot when expressing yourself to others. Let's look back at the first question and think about what kind of day you had.

Let's say that you rolled out of your bed with extreme reluctance, your coffee tasted like mud, you had no hot water, your dog was behaving like Cujo and ripped all your furniture, a robber snuck into your house and stole your breakfast and went to the bathroom on your kitchen floor, and you missed your bus. You arrive late for English 101 and the professor wants you to summarize your morning in a sentence. What do you write? You may not go into grand detail but you may write something similar to this: *My morning was challenging because unexpected and unfortunate events stunted my appreciation for my life at the moment.* Do you think this is an appropriate summarization of your day so far? Discuss why or why not with a partner. To help, think about these qualities that all summaries should have:

- Must contain the main points of a piece or event. Stating the author's most important idea is crucial for capturing what the author is trying to express. The main idea will most likely be found in the thesis statement.
- Will be shorter than the original writing or explanation (this is unlike paraphrasing which requires you to put an original piece in your own words and is just as long as the original; think of "summing up" when you hear "summary").
- Will accurately represent the original meaning.
- Look for topic sentences to help set a framework or outline for your summary.
- Be sure that your ideas are in order.
- Take time to differentiate important information that would make your summary incomplete if not included, and information that is trivial or not essential to paint an accurate picture of what a passage is explaining.

For more information about summarizing, please visit http://owl.english.purdue.edu/owl/

Student Example A

Recall	Notes (in your own words)

CHAPTER: 4   **DATE:** Feb 3

Types of
Leadership

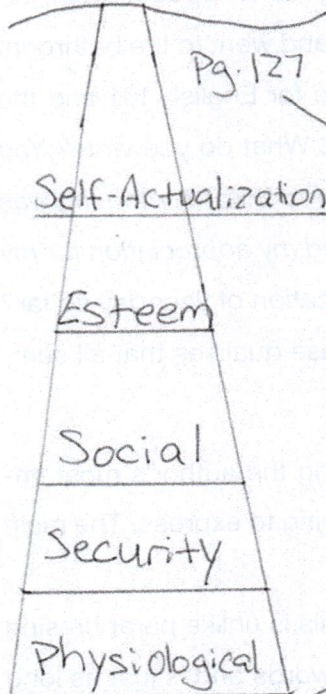

Pg. 127

Self-Actualization

Esteem

Social

Security

Physiological

Pg. 122

Why do some
believe in Theroy X
and others in
Theroy Y?

Motivational Theories
- Explain how human relations
  affects motivation.

Maslow's Hierarchy of Needs
(Motivational theroy)
1) Physiological Needs → Survival Food
                                    Shelter
2) Security Needs → Stability & protection
3) Social Needs → Friendship & companions
4) Esteem Needs → Status & recognition
5) Self-Actualization → self-fulfillment
   * Dev. by Abram Maslow
   * MEET LOWER NEEDS 1st

Theory X → holds that people are
           naturally irresponsible.

Theory Y → holds that people are
           naturally self motivated &
           responsible
   * Dev. by Douglas McGregor
   * What type of leader you are
     is determined by which theroy
     you believe in.

SUMMARY / POSSIBLE TEST QUESTIONS

Motivational theroies explain how & why people are
motivated. 2 motivational Theories are
Maslow's hierarchy of needs & Theroy X & Y.

In Defense of Food
Chapter 4: Food Science's Golden Age

Golden Age Food Science	Scientists were making popular food products contain more nutrients or so we thought. **OUTCOME:** Food with labels saying: low-fat no-cholesterol Foods with additives
Adulterants	**Adulterants Def:** Chemical that should not be combined with other substances; lessen effectiveness of a substance and can be harmful.
1988	**Year of Eating Oat Bran** • Succeeded in getting oat bran into almost all processed food • Set the pattern for manipulating food
Lipophobia	**Lipophobia def:** avoidance of eating fatty foods
Can food be changed to fit nutritional standards?	*RESULT* **Pigs-** breeding of leaner pigs creating "the NEW white meat" reducing saturated fat intake. **Chickens-** higher levels of omega-3's in yolk by feeding flaxseed to hens
Whole foods in competition with nutritionalism	The sales of whole foods rise and fall as changes are made in the nutritional world because it's much harder to genetically engineer their make-up. Unlike processed foods which can be reformulated at any given time. **EX: Atkins Diet 2003** Breads and pastas were redesigned to fit the diet bearing "low carb" labels; while fresh veggies were left untouched on the engineering end and also on the market shelves.
"Good nutrient" marketing treatment	**Pomegranate-** antioxidants protect against cancer and erectile dysfunction **Walnut-** omega-3 fatty acids act as a defense mechanism for heart disease

Summary
The Golden Age of food science was the start of manipulating the foods we consume to fit the nutrition profile. Just because pork is leaner and higher levels of omega-3 can be found in egg yolks doesn't necessarily mean they are better for you. You receive more nutrients and can prevent disease by consuming natural foods like a walnut.

CHAPTER: **DATE:**

Summary

Critical Thinking

Critical thinking is well, critical in your college journey. Problem-solving, time management, and most if not all decisions are best made when students use critical thinking. Critical thinking is taking information at its face value in determining its usefulness. Critical thinkers investigate information to determine its validity, reliability, and accuracy and as much as possible take emotions out of the equation. Philosopher John Dewey stated "Attitude is a key ingredient in how we think". Attitude includes open-mindedness, wholeheartedness, and responsibility.

Open-mindedness is a person's willingness to look at information and not make judgments, even when the information does not fit into their system of processing material. Open-mindedness will stretch one's view of life, allowing us to grow. Open-mindedness is difficult because often information conflicts with our values, morals, and sense of right and wrong, but open-mindedness does not mean take information and make it yours. Open-mindedness is processing information to determine whether it will fit into your present system or whether your present system needs to change so the information will fit.

Wholeheartedness is related to a student's passion for knowledge. That is to say, when an individual is passionate, that passion will drive them to find out and to gain more and more of what they crave.

Responsibility is a moral attitude that accepts the logical consequences of a particular belief or behavior. Again Dewey states, "To be intellectually responsible is to consider the consequences of a projected step; it means to be willing to adopt these consequences when they follow reasonably from any position already taken. Intellectual responsibility secures integrity; that is to say, consistency and harmony in belief". Being responsible for our thoughts and behaviors no matter the consequences will compel us to be more aware of the decisions we make and how they impact us.

Open-mindedness + Wholeheartedness + Responsibility = Critical Thinking

A Critical Thinker should:

Think actively

Think of examples that prove the statement

Think of examples that disprove the statement

Think of specific things that support the different perspectives

Seek the views of others on this topic

Draw your own conclusions with appropriate supporting facts and arguments.

A **Critical Thinker** can use four different steps to arrive at a thoughtful conclusion:

1. Construct questions to independently clarify the problems being dealt with.

2. Organize and develop plans to form a logical argument; identify the supporting evidence that relates to the question as well as the opposing evidence.

3. Test each piece of evidence on both sides for truthfulness and context.

4. Develop a logical argument based on the evidence that will prove or disprove the claim being made.

Stages of Critical Thinking

1. **The Unreflective Thinker**—we are unaware of significant problems in our thinking.

2. **The Challenged Thinker**—we become aware of problems in our thinking.

3. **The Beginning Thinker**—we try to improve, but without regular practice.

4. **The Practicing Thinker**—we recognize the necessity of regular practice.

5. **The Advanced Thinker**—we advance in accordance with our practice.

6. **The Master Thinker**—skilled and insightful thinking become second nature to us.

Concept Cards

What you will need:

➤ 4x6 or 5x7 (the larger the better)

➤ Color pens, pencils, or markers

➤ Textbook, lecture notes, etc

© RetroClipArt, 2012. Used under license from Shutterstock, Inc.

Everyone has used flashcards at least once in their life. If you have tried them in college you may have been unsatisfied with the results come time for an exam. A typical flashcard is made with one word on a side and just the definition on the other, which limits the learner. You may know the definition by heart after studying it several times, but you might not understand what it means. By using concept cards, you can put more information on the card to better understand a term. Not only can you fit a lot of information onto the card, they are easy to carry! You can keep them on you and when you have free time, pull them out and review.

Three Steps to Making and Studying a Concept Card

Step 1: Filtering out the important information. Go over your lecture notes and textbook and compare the bold or italicized words and headings. Professors don't tell you everything in lecture, so it's best to refer to the book to further understand key details.

Step 2: Making the memory cards. Put a word, words or a concept on the front of the card and the supporting information on the other. While you're doing this, make sure to say it out loud to help you remember.

Step 3: Studying the cards. If you need to review the cards in order first, then do so, after that SHUFFLE, SHUFFLE, SHUFFLE! Only pick 5–7 cards at a time, flipping them front to back when reviewing them. Mark a check (if you got the card right) or an X (if you got the card wrong) on the upper right hand corner of the card. Once you get three check marks in a row you know it!

Look on the next page to see an example of a concept card.

Example of a Concept Card

DNA
Helicase

Def: breaks H bonds between the 2
nucleotide strands of DNA

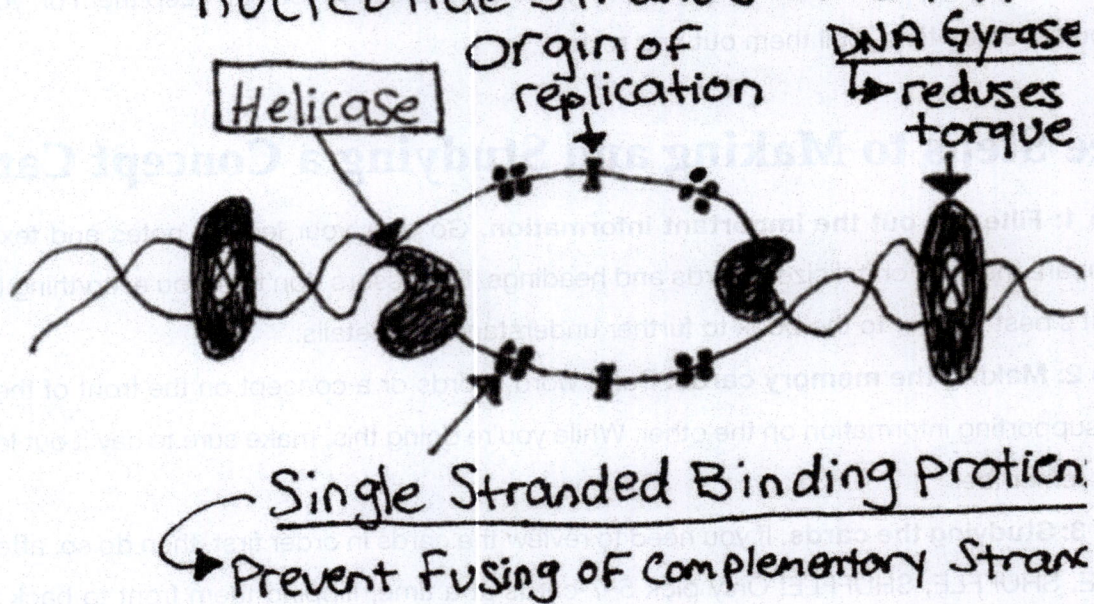

Orgin of
replication

DNA Gyrase
→reduses
torque

Helicase

Single Stranded Binding Protien
→Prevent Fusing of Complementary Stran

Note Swap Activity

Directions: "Grade" your peers' notes or your own notes using this quick assessment.

Component	YES	NO
Are the notes legible?		
Is there a date at the top?		
Are the main headings easy to find?		
Are key points underlined/highlighted?		
Can you find any examples?		
Are things abbreviated or paraphrased?		
Are there any diagrams, drawings, page #s?		
Is there any coding (arrows, ? , ! . #)		
Are the notes in a designated binder/notebook?		
Are textbook notes added to lecture notes?		

Total YES:_____

Multiply the number of YES's times ten. Highest score is 100.

What New Components Will You Include in Your Own Notes?

1.

2.

3.

The Fold Out Strategy

The Fold Out strategy is a brand new approach to studying! Students can use the Fold Out strategy in two ways:

1. **Before class** while skimming the reading. Key words and definitions are written in the KEY WORD column. Once in class, the student can listen for the key words and add what the professor said about the term. After class, the student completes the ME column.

2. **After class** while reviewing notes. Add to the guide any additional textbook information to fill in the gaps and elaborate on the information.

In both cases, this new strategy helps improve student comprehension of the material. Since it is in a handy format, the Fold Outs are easy to take with you to study on the go. Make one or several for the upcoming exam. Some students prefer to make one for each lecture class. Be sure to make several copies of the Fold Out and keep them in your binder.

How to Fold the Fold Out:

1. Look at the side that says KEY WORDS, PROFESSOR, and ME.

2. Fold the ME column over so that you bend the crease and can still read the KEY WORD column.

3. Next, fold over the KEY WORD column and make a crease. It will start to look like an envelope.

4. Complete the information on the back of the Fold Out so that you know when your next exam will be, what it will cover and your goal grade. Also, complete the information on the flap so you know what content is contained in the guide.

What Goes in Each Section:

KEY WORDS	TEXTBOOK	PROFESSOR	ME
• Bold terms • Italicized terms • Terms the professor repeated more than once • Terms you are unfamiliar with	• Definitions of the key words • Page numbers • Diagrams • Examples • Additional facts	• Examples mentioned in class • Information not covered in the text • Class notes	• Mnemonic devices/ acronyms • Helpful rhymes/ stories that tie the new information to prior knowledge • Notes in your own words

TEXTBOOK

TEST DATE: _____

GOAL GRADE: _____

CHAPTERS TO STUDY:

WHAT IS THIS THING?

1.) THE KEY WORD COLUMN: Spend a few minutes skimming the material in your textbook that will be covered in your next class. Use your class syllabus as a guide. Find any words in bold, italics, main headings, and so on that stand out as important. Simply record these words in the key word column and then...

2.) THE TEXTBOOK COLUMN: Fold on the line between the PROFESSOR and ME columns so that the TEXTBOOK column magically appears next to the KEY WORD column. *In your own words* write a brief summary of the key terms that you selected. Now you are ready for a fulfilling lecture class.

3.) THE PROFESSOR COLUMN: You decide... you can keep the PROFESSOR column open during class or you can take notes the usual way and then transfer what was said in class onto your fold-out after class. Did your professor mention any of the words that you selected? What did the professor say about the key term?

4.) THE ME COLUMN: Now it is your turn. What do you need this column for? More examples, drawings, extra space, to refer to your own life experiences, or maybe even for a mnemonic device or memory aid.

HELPFUL HINTS:

Adapt to your *own* needs. You'll never do the textbook column after class? That's okay, do it afterwards!

Start these early... they'll be helpful study guides.

Draw lines between key terms and/or use color-coding to help you stay focused and on task!

Take them with you on the bus, home, or wherever and use the fold-out a few minutes a day!

CHAPTER/CONCEPT:

KEY WORDS	PROFESSOR	ME

Discussion: Organization, Studying, and Note-Taking

Whenever I am in class, I tend to write down every single word the professor says. How do I determine what is important to write down?

– Angel

It takes me ten minutes to find anything! This makes me miss out on taking notes. Help!

– Derrick

My exam is in a week. I am used to cramming, but I want to start studying earlier. How do I get started?

– Robin

CPSIA information can be obtained at www.ICGtesting.com
Printed in the USA
LVOW05s0522060815

448820LV00003BA/3/P